STEP UP

STEP UP

BECOMING THE LEADER GOD MADE YOU TO BE

DENISE VANECK

ZONDERVAN.com/
AUTHORTRACKER
follow your favorite authors

ZONDERVAN

STEP UP

Previously published as *Leadership 101*

This title is also available as a Zondervan ebook.
Visit www.zondervan.com/ebooks.

Requests for information should be addressed to:

Zondervan, Grand Rapids, Michigan 49530

Library of Congress Cataloguing-in-Publication Data

CIP information is available: 978-0-310-70000-5

Cover design: Micah Kandros
Cover photography: Veer
Interior design: Mark Novelli, Imago Media

Printed in the United States of America

13 14 15 16 /DCI/ 20 19 18 17 16 15 14 13 12 11 10 9 8 7 6 5 4 3 2 1

CONTENTS

INTRODUCTION

"And David shepherded them with integrity of heart;
with skillful hands he led them."
—Psalm 78:72

David is one of my heroes. He was a great leader who was able to face impossible obstacles and persecution with great courage. He turned a small group of ragamuffin outlaws into "mighty men," and he grew from shepherd boy to king. He rejoiced, grieved, triumphed, failed, and worshiped with all of his heart. He was a real man with real passions and desires, real sin, and real troubles. At the end of his life, he was called a man after God's own heart. He gave his life to serve a real God.

Asaph, who wrote Psalm 78, describes David's leadership as having two components: integrity and skill. My dream is to train young men and women with hearts like David's to lead others with integrity and skill. It is my prayer that this manual will flow from the heart of God and into the hearts of young leaders—you! I pray all who use this manual will experience God in new ways and emerge changed—challenged and ready for the tasks God assigns to them.

Like snowflakes, no two leaders are alike. Your leadership DNA is unique and perfectly crafted by a creative, sovereign God. This book should be used not as a final authority on the topic of leadership but as a springboard to exploring God's plan for your own leadership. It is my desire that what you read and write in this book will stimulate your thinking and prompt you to further study of these topics.

This manual is divided into two main parts. The first takes you through an exploration of the integrity—or integration—of your heart; the second focuses on the various skills effective leaders must sharpen before they can positively impact the people they're leading. Each chapter builds on the one before it, and the final chapter wraps up everything God has taught you throughout the book.

Each chapter is comprised of several parts. In addition to the reading, which is intended to increase your knowledge and stimulate your thinking, there are questions for you to ponder and answer. (And please do answer them; this is as much a workbook as it is a book to be read.) Feel free to write your answers in the blank spaces below each of the questions so you can refer to them in the future. You'll also find suggestions for how you can "take it deeper." These sections will expand your resources beyond the pages of this book and help you further explore the covered topics. Finally, there are journaling exercises at the end of each chapter. I encourage you to use these "journaling snapshots" as a way to develop journaling as an ongoing spiritual discipline in your life. When you're finished reading part of a chapter, go to the end and work on one or even a couple of the journaling snapshot questions. Don't rush through this process! Spend all the time you need recording your thoughts, prayers, and feelings in the presence of God. While it's ideal to finish the journaling snapshots at the same time you finish a chapter, it's not necessary. You can move on to the next chapter even if you haven't finished the previous chapter's journaling snapshots. The important thing is to journal consistently. It's my prayer that you'll grow to love and relish this time of communing with God as you go through the book.

I pray your journey into the world of leadership will be a blessing to you and will bring glory to our Almighty King.

—Denise VanEck

PART ONE

And David shepherded them with integrity of heart…

■ CHAPTER ONE

WHAT IS LEADERSHIP?

Peter ate heartily as the conversation continued around him. Some were talking about the authoritative way that Jesus had overturned the trading tables in the court of the Gentiles. Others were making plans for the future now that the tide had turned for them.

Unnoticed in the midst of the hubbub, the Master rose and made his way out of the room. He reappeared several minutes later, his chest bare and a towel wrapped around his waist. Walking deliberately over to the corner, he poured fresh water into a clay basin. As Jesus picked up the basin, an abrupt silence fell upon the group.

Peter wondered what the Master was doing now. Jesus looked for all the world like a common servant. He knelt in front of Judas and motioned for him to place his foot in the basin. Judas looked terribly uncomfortable as the Master began to wash his feet. As the Master continued, Judas' discomfort turned into agitation.

All eyes in the room were fixed on Jesus. What was this all about? The men watched Jesus pour a dipper of water over Judas' feet and then tenderly wipe them dry with the towel he had wrapped around his waist. The Master carried the basin to the next person, John. As he bent down to wash John's feet, he spoke lovingly: "You do not realize now what I am doing, but later you will understand."

Peter was repelled by the scene. This was their Master, the one they were calling the new King of Israel, and he was on his knees washing their feet as if he were the lowliest servant in the household! There was no way he, Peter, would lower himself to do the job of a common servant.

Peter was next in line, and he could see it coming. But Peter wanted none of it. Embarrassment aside, it just wasn't right! No man—least of all a man with the importance of the Master—should have to wash his followers' feet. That's what servants were for.

The master dried John's feet and pushed the basin toward Peter. "No," Peter said firmly, looking straight into the Master's eyes. "You will never wash my feet."

Jesus looked up at Peter's face. Gently and patiently he said, "Unless I wash you, you have no part with me."

The room was quiet. Outside, the laughter of children could be heard. Peter sat stiffly. He knew he must be missing something. Then, slowly at first, past conversations came to Peter's mind. *The last shall be first. Except you become as a child. He who would be great among you must be your servant.* Illumination began to flood Peter. This wasn't really about washing dirty feet. It was about humility, about taking the lesser path, even when glory was in sight. Now he understood what the Master was doing! "Peter, if I do not wash your feet, you can have no part with me," the Master repeated.

Peter's reply was barely audible to the others: "Then, Lord, not just my feet but my hands and my head as well."

As Peter spoke, the resistance seemed to seep out of him. Peter sat quietly and allowed Jesus to minister to him while the other disciples watched in studied silence.

Finally, the Master was done. He rose to his feet, rubbing his back. Then he spoke to all the disciples: "Do you understand what I have done for you? You call me 'Teacher' and 'Lord,' and rightly so, for that is what I am. Now that I, your Lord the Teacher, have washed your feet, you also should wash one another's feet. I have set you an example that you should do as I have done for you."

—from *The Leadership Paradox* by Denny Gunderson

LEADERSHIP

Okay, you've heard the word, but what does it mean? Leadership is a term that defies description. According to John Maxwell, a renowned leadership expert, there are currently 350 working definitions of the word in current literature. Three hundred and fifty definitions! Still, most people say it's a term they understand. But do we really? Let's play with this idea for a little while.

How would you define the word leadership?

"Leadership is influence."
—JOHN C. MAXWELL, **DEVELOPING THE LEADER WITHIN YOU**

Pretty hard, isn't it? The trouble is, almost every time you settle on a definition, you can think of an exception to it. Look at the definitions in the outer margin. Circle the one(s) you agree with most.

"Leadership to me is a very simple thing. Creating consensus and aligning people behind a vision, not just telling them what needs to be done, but this is the key—why it should be done. Create an environment in which people WANT to do the job, rather than HAVE to do the job—that is leadership."
—HORST SCHULTZ (PRESIDENT AND CEO OF THE RITZ-CARLTON HOTELS), AS QUOTED IN THE **EXPLORER E-NEWSLETTER** (JANUARY 31, 2000)

"Leadership is a process of giving purpose (meaningful direction) to collective effort, and causing willing effort to be expended to achieve purpose."
—T. OWEN JACOBS AND ELLIOT JAQUES, "MILITARY EXECUTIVE LEADERSHIP" IN **MEASURES OF LEADERSHIP** (BY KENNETH E. CLARK AND MIRIAM B. CLARK, EDS.)

"Leading is establishing direction and influencing others to follow that direction. Leadership is the art of mobilizing others to want to struggle for shared aspirations."
—JAMES M. KOUZES AND BARRY Z. POSNER, **THE LEADERSHIP CHALLENGE**

"Leadership is a development of a clear and complete system of expectations in order to identify, evoke, and use the strengths of all resources in the organization, the most important of which is people."
—JOE D. BATTEN, **TOUGH-MINDED LEADERSHIP**

TAKE IT DEEPER

DEFINE LEADERSHIP

Do an Internet search for the word *leadership.* How many sites did you find?

Do any of them define leadership?

Write out three of the best definitions you found online—

1.

2.

3.

LEADERS IN MY LIFE

Think about the people you consider leaders. List the first three who come to mind.

1.

2.

3.

What makes you consider each person you listed a leader? After each name list the leadership qualities you've observed in that person.

List three people who've had the most impact on your life. (This could include people you don't know personally.)

1.

2.

3.

Beside each of these three names list the person's qualities that have influenced you the most.

Were the people you included on your first list different from the ones on your second list? If so, when you thought of leaders, why didn't you think of people in your life who have influenced you? Have you bought into the world's perspective that leadership is about being in charge? We often believe leaders are the ones at the top. Of course, that can be part of what leadership is—but don't be lulled into thinking that's what it's all about.

One of the people I'd include on my second list is Sharon, a neighbor of mine while I was growing up. When I was a sophomore in high school, I reached my lowest point in a string of poor choices and needed to live away from home for a while. Sharon and her husband took me in. Sharon changed my life. She loved me despite the choices I'd made. She set clear boundaries for me—certain behaviors had to begin, certain friends had to go. Then she did the most amazing thing. She put her arms around me and wept with me as I grieved the loss of the things I had to let go.

As I tried to make some hard changes during the next few months, Sharon kept reminding me about my incredible future and the things I could do well; she encouraged me to step out and take some risks. She continually spoke truth to me about who God was and how he viewed me. Sharon was a housewife with three kids in Ada, Michigan. You'll probably never meet her or hear her name on the news, but Sharon was one of the most powerful leaders in my life. I wanted to be just like her. Her life and her actions influenced me to make some major changes—changes that in part led me to the place where I am today. That's great leadership!

CHARACTER VERSUS SKILLS

There are those who say leadership is about your character or who you are, while others say leadership is defined by your skills or what you do.

People who defend the first perspective point out the importance of integrity, charisma, and other internal characteristics. They say who you are affects what you do. A perfect example is Mother Teresa. (If you don't know much about her, check out www.drini.com/motherteresa.) She's remembered as one of the most respected and influential women of the twentieth century solely based on her ability to live out her personal convictions. Did she possess a strong, commanding persona? Did she influence people with her charm and charisma? Not at all! She was a quiet, soft-spoken little woman who was ordinary on the outside. Nevertheless, she influenced thousands to minister to the poor and dying of Calcutta and places like it around the world. The strength of her character made her an incredible leader.

On the other side, there are many who believe the quality of one's leadership is determined by one's leadership skills. This is where powers of communication, persuasion, knowledge, and experience come in. Former President Bill Clinton is a great example of one who is seen as a great leader because of his skills. He is said to be an incredible listener, remarkably skilled at remembering detail, persuasive, and highly intelligent. He attained the highest position of leadership in the world, mostly due to his skills in the area of leadership, yet spurred a national debate on the importance of a leader's character. Many people thought Clinton's private moral failures were irrelevant to his position as the leader of this country—essentially that his heart attitude wasn't important. Those people contend that Clinton was elected for his skill, not his heart. Others believe his character was totally relevant to his ability to command respect as a leader. So who is right? I believe the answer is found in a verse that will be foundational to your study of leadership: "And David shepherded them with integrity of heart, with skillful hands he led them" (Psalm 78:72).

For years the secular leadership community has argued about the values of skill and character. Volumes have been written in dozens and dozens of leadership books expounding on the importance of one or the other. But the greatest manual on leadership was written thousands of years ago, and it contains about every answer to about every question you could ever ask about the topic! The Bible contains at least 170 direct references to leading and many more stories that illustrate leadership—both good and bad examples. So how does God's Word define leadership? According to Psalm 78:72, good leadership requires both integrity of heart and skill, in equal measure.

INTEGRITY OF HEART

What comes to mind when you think of the word *integrity?* Most of us leap to words such as *honesty* or phrases such as "man of his word." Those are good definitions, but integrity literally means "to integrate" or bring many parts together.

Having integrity of heart means bringing together all the parts of who you are. It means having one *self*—being the same person whether you are alone or in a crowd, at school or with your family. As you will discover in the next few chapters, there are many parts to your self.

News Flash: You have a distinct, unique personality and temperament. You have a unique pathway in which you relate to God. Your experiences and influences have uniquely shaped you. You have physical, emotional, intellectual, and spiritual parts of your self. Understanding these things and bringing them into unity is key to having what we call integrity of heart.

David had integrity of heart. I want integrity of heart—and I believe you do, too. The journey takes effort, perseverance, and much courage; but as David's life shows us, the results are very much worth the effort.

SKILLFUL HANDS

In our quest to grow in very important heart issues, it's also important to recognize the necessity of basic leadership skills. Throughout his lifetime David's leadership was challenged by his skills in five major areas: listening, communicating, managing conflict, learning from failure, and raising up other leaders. Many godly leaders have suffered through unnecessary failures of leadership due to poor skills, especially in these key areas. There are, of course, many other skills that leaders must develop as well, but I'm convinced that mastery of the "big five" is absolutely essential for any leader's true success.

What Does It Mean?

In•teg•ri•ty \ in-te'-grə -tē \ *n* in the quality or state of being complete or undivided

Sometimes Leading "Right" Is Wrong

In the past, and as recently as a year ago, my ideas of true leadership were skewed. I thought being a leader meant being the receiver of glory and the holder of control. Believing I had the gift of being a natural leader, I found myself taking positions and accepting roles that put my abilities and me in the spotlight. Because I was so scared of failure, I spent many hours planning, organizing, and replanning in order to earn the extra attention of being the outstanding leader. Sure, I earned the respect of the people I led, and occasionally I would win the praise I was hungry for, but it wasn't as rewarding or as glamorous as I'd pictured it. It felt fake. Eventually I realized it felt that way because I was doing it for all the wrong reasons. I wasn't leading because I was passionate about the cause but rather because I was passionate about the control. If I've learned anything since then, it's that leadership isn't about you. It's about those you are leading and where you're leading them. Leadership is a behind-the-scenes sacrifice that results in a great sense of accomplishment when you view the successes of others. I've learned that rather than leadership being equal to dictatorship, it should be synonymous with servanthood.

—Beth Groner, age 19

HEART TO HANDS

It's no accident that in Psalm 78:72 *heart* comes before *skill*. The Hebrew word *leb* (pronounced "lave") means "heart." The literal translation is "the source of man." A person's *leb* is the source of her passions, knowledge, and character. It's kind of like the spring that feeds the river that runs into the oceans. If you pollute the spring, then all the water flowing out of it will also be polluted. Are you familiar with Proverbs 4:23? "Above all else, guard your heart, for it affects everything you do" (NLT). Even the most skilled leader will be ineffective—or worse, destructive—when the heart is allowed to turn from God. Adolf Hitler was a powerfully influential leader who changed the history of the world, but his evil heart determined the course of his leadership. Can you imagine how many people's lives would be radically different today if Hitler had led with integrity of heart?

What other characteristics or skills should a good leader possess? Here you will find a list of words that describe some characteristics of a good leader. Identify whether the word describes an attribute of the heart, the hands (a skill), or both, and then rate yourself on how much you possess that particular trait.

TRAIT	HEART/ HANDS /BOTH	1 (HAVEN'T GOT A CLUE) TO 5 (GOT IT WRAPPED UP)
Integrity	______________	1 2 3 4 5
Intelligence	______________	1 2 3 4 5
Honesty	______________	1 2 3 4 5
Passion	______________	1 2 3 4 5
Genuineness	______________	1 2 3 4 5
Courage	______________	1 2 3 4 5
Persistence	______________	1 2 3 4 5
Good Communicator	______________	1 2 3 4 5
Approachable	______________	1 2 3 4 5
Imaginative	______________	1 2 3 4 5
Insightful	______________	1 2 3 4 5
Humble	______________	1 2 3 4 5
Learner	______________	1 2 3 4 5
Role Model	______________	1 2 3 4 5
Committed	______________	1 2 3 4 5
Visionary	______________	1 2 3 4 5
Sincere	______________	1 2 3 4 5
Good Listener	______________	1 2 3 4 5
Delegates	______________	1 2 3 4 5
People Skills	______________	1 2 3 4 5
Authentic	______________	1 2 3 4 5
Influential	______________	1 2 3 4 5
Knowledgeable about Task	______________	1 2 3 4 5
Decision Maker	______________	1 2 3 4 5
Servant	______________	1 2 3 4 5

I have a hunch you may finish evaluating yourself in these areas and decide that because you didn't score fives in every area, then you must not be cut out for leadership. Go back and reread the story at the beginning of the chapter. It shows that one of the things that made Jesus an incredible leader was his ability to see beyond the weaknesses and inexperience of his disciples and to bring out their true potential. Jesus knows Peter will be the rock on which he will build the church (Matthew 16:18); he also knows Peter needs to learn about servanthood and humility first. So Jesus patiently and wisely *models* it for him.

You may not possess many of the characteristics or skills needed for leadership right now, but you can certainly learn them. Notice how Peter pays attention to the things Jesus says and does. Peter is willing to learn and change. And what does Jesus say to Peter when he knows Peter finally understands what Jesus is trying to teach him about leadership? "Now that I, your Lord and Teacher, have washed your feet, you also should wash one another's feet. I have set you an example that you should do as I have done for you" (John 13:14-15).

THE "GIRL ISSUE"—CAN GIRLS LEAD?

"Women should remain silent in the churches. They are not allowed to speak, but must be in submission, as the Law says."
—1 Corinthians 14:34

"A woman should learn in quietness and full submission. I do not permit a woman to teach or to have authority over a man; she must be silent."
—1 Timothy 2:11-12

These verses are often referred to as "problem passages" in discussion regarding the roles of women in the church. They are certainly hard to read, especially for girls. It's difficult to understand how Paul, who wrote these words, could seem so disrespectful toward women when he clearly valued the roles of many women in his ministry. Some very wise people have studied this issue and concluded it's God's will that females not be allowed to be leaders in the church. Other equally wise people have studied the same passages and concluded the opposite. It's a topic worth studying and praying about on your own.

However, it's important to note that when Paul talks about the spiritual gift of leadership, he never says it's only given to guys. The Holy Spirit distributes all the gifts to all believers, not just to one gender or the other. Girls have a great contribution to make in the world. They shouldn't be disrespected or disqualified from leadership just because of their gender, and they shouldn't use their gender as an excuse to get out of the hard work of leadership, either.

Girls, if your church doesn't allow women to serve as pastors or teachers, then you can still find ways to exercise your gift of leadership. God may be calling you to use your gifts outside the church. Don't give up or give in!

Please make sure you watch, listen, stay teachable, and practice the things you are learning. You may be tempted to give in to pride, resist change, or put only a minimum of effort into your study of leadership. Please resist with all of your strength. God wants to use YOU to advance his kingdom.

"When being is divorced from doing, pious thoughts become an adequate substitute for washing dirty feet."
—BRENNAN MANNING, **ABBA'S CHILD**

JOURNALING SNAPSHOTS

KEEPING A RECORD OF YOUR JOURNEY

A friend once said to me, "If the creator of the universe said something just to you, wouldn't you want to remember it?" Of course I would! But too often I don't take the time to do it. It's so easy to stay busy and not take the time to talk with God, isn't it?

A lot of people use journaling to encounter God in a really personal way. Keeping a journal of your spiritual journey is kind of like taking pictures on a vacation. When you look back at the photo album of your trip, not only are you reminded of places or events you may have forgotten ("Oh yeah! Look how cool the sunset was that day!"), but you can also relive parts of the trip through those pictures. Similarly, when you keep a journal, you record some of your conversations and interactions with God so you can look back later and remember the things he's taught you and see how you've grown.

"Neo, sooner or later you're going to realize just as I did that there's a difference between knowing the path and walking the path."
—MORPHEUS, **THE MATRIX**

Even after writing this book, I know that what I have to offer you is nothing compared to what God wants to teach you. This book is really designed as a launching pad. I hope you learn some stuff from the chapters I've written, but I'm totally convinced that most of the best learning you will do will come during your quiet times with God as you jump into his Word and spend time talking with him.

So please take the time to get yourself a journal of some sort. It can be a notebook, a scrapbook, or a special journal with unlined pages—whatever! Just find something you can devote specifically to this journey. Each chapter will end with exercises to get you started. Don't rush through this process! Spend all the time you need recording your thoughts, prayers, and feelings in the presence of God. While it's ideal to finish the journaling snapshots at the same time you finish a chapter, it's not necessary. You can move on to the next chapter even if you haven't finished the previous chapter's journaling snapshots. The important thing is to journal consistently.

And you should feel free to adapt the exercises to whatever seems right to you. If you want to illustrate your responses instead of using words—please do. If you want to add poetry or music—go for it. Just get into the conversation with God and take those snapshots!

DAY 1

Read 1 Chronicles 28. Solomon is a young, inexperienced leader called to a huge task—rebuilding God's temple. So Solomon's father, King David, gives his son several specific words of instruction and encouragement. In your Bible underline the words of instruction and encouragement that you feel apply to you in your leadership journey. Then in your journal write out a prayer to God telling him what those words mean to you. Be honest about your fears, your hopes, and your dreams.

DAY 2

Read Psalm 119:1-24. As we study the heart of the leader, we must stay focused on the instructions God gives us for taking care of our hearts. In your own words rewrite this psalm as a prayer to God.

DAY 3

Read Philippians 2:1-11. Consider what this passage could mean to a leader and write down your thoughts. Focus on the third verse. Are you challenged by it? Ask God specifically how you can do a better job of living this out.

DAY 4

Read Jeremiah 17:5-10. There is a clear contrast between relying on people (ourselves included) and relying on God for our wisdom and strength. Write out a prayer to God confessing the ways you wrongly rely on yourself or others and ask for his help.

DAY 5

Read Proverbs 2:1-10. One of the most important qualities of a good leader is wisdom. We often hope it will just drop on us as rain does, but this passage tells us that we must search for wisdom as we would hunt for silver or hidden treasure. Reflect for a moment on how you are searching for wisdom and understanding. What does "call[ing] out for insight and cry[ing] aloud for understanding" look like in your life? As you ponder this, record your thoughts in your journal.

■CHAPTER TWO

WHAT KIND OF LEADER AM I?

A couple of years ago I set out on a little journey with my son. He was taking a plane out of Chicago to go visit his big brother out East. The airport is a three-hour drive from our house, but I decided to leave early so we could have time to do some last-minute shopping and get some of Nick's favorite Chicago pizza. I'd found some directions to the airport on the Internet and printed them out to guide me on the journey. So six hours before his flight was scheduled to take off, we left home.

Everything went perfectly until we were about 20 miles from the exit, and the directions told me to get off the highway. Traffic came to a standstill. Ninety minutes later we arrived at the exit. I didn't see an airport sign, but it was definitely the exit my directions told me to take. That was the moment I realized I didn't have what I really needed—a map! All I had were the written directions. I decided I really had no choice but to follow them. I'll spare you the gory details of the next two hours. As it turned out, the directions took us by way of the shortest route, which was a road with stoplights at every corner and bumper-to-bumper traffic. Instead of traveling a few more miles on the highway, we took a shortcut into standstill traffic. Not only did we not get to shop or eat pizza—but we also missed Nick's flight! If I'd brought a map, I would have seen how the highways connected near the airport. That day I decided I'd never go on another journey without bringing a map.

You're going to need a map for your journey into leadership, too. I could give you directions, but you'll be much better off if you study the map on your own, familiarizing yourself with where you are and where you want to go.

Don't rush through the upcoming sections. Take your time and try to think about each one as deeply as you can. You might be tempted to ask someone else to tell you how to answer some of the questions, but please don't. Later on it will be helpful to get feedback and observations from others to help you fill in some things or to understand how accurately you perceive yourself. But for now just trust yourself and the Holy Spirit to do the work.

MILESTONES

Before you can really tell where you want to go, it's helpful to take a look back at where you've been. Your experiences are part of you. As you take this journey into leadership from an integrated heart, you'll bring all that you've learned and become as a result of the milestones in your life. Let's identify what those are. In this exercise you are going to create a time line of your life so far.

Begin by grabbing your journal and a pen. We'll take the first 10 years of your life in blocks of five. In your journal write YEARS 0-5 and make a chronological list of the major events that *changed life for you*. They can be things such as births of siblings, moves, accidents, meeting a new friend, parents divorcing, or whatever was significant to your life. When you've finished, do the same for years 6-10 and then for two-year blocks after that (11-12, 13-14, and so on). Now go back and look at each entry on the list. Try to come up with at least one word for each entry that describes what changed in you or what you learned from that experience. It can be positive or negative—or even both.

For example, one of the milestones in my life was taking a confirmation class at church when I was 11 years old. I realized I had to decide for myself what I believed about God and whether I was going to follow him or not. When I entered that event on my timeline, I put the word *faith* next to it. Another event on my timeline is when I was 15 years old and falsely accused of stealing some purses at a party. Everyone I thought was my friend abandoned me. It was a horrible time, but I learned a lot about myself. I realized how important it was to me that people like me—and what it felt like to be the outcast. I learned sometimes it's impossible to defend myself, and instead I have to depend on God to do it for me. I actually learned lots of stuff during that time, but you get the idea. Next to that event on my timeline I wrote the words *courage, strength, humility, dependence on God.*

Keep going until your list catches up with your life today. Later in the chapter you'll use this list to create a timeline to help you map out how your experiences are integrated with the other aspects of your self that you'll discover in this chapter.

YOUR PROVISIONS

SPIRITUAL GIFTS

One of the very cool perks of following Christ is that when we give our lives to him, we get presents! In the New Testament they're called spiritual gifts. In his letters to the churches, Paul talks a lot about the church functioning as a "body." Just as your physical body possesses many parts, the body of Christ has many different parts, and they all have different jobs to do. We are given special abilities (or gifts) to get those jobs done. Some of the gifts are very practical (teaching, encouraging, serving, giving, leadership, administration), and some are more mystical (wisdom, faith, words of knowledge, healing, tongues).

We all like presents, right? True gifts are expressions of love and affection, freely given with no strings attached. Who doesn't love that? There is one thing you need to know about these presents, though—something that makes them way different than the presents you usually get. That cool pair of shoes your mom bought for your birthday was all about YOU; they were for you to enjoy and to keep for yourself. But the presents you receive from the Holy Spirit—your spiritual gifts—are given to you for everyone else. That's right! God doesn't give these gifts for us to hoard and enjoy for our own benefit. Each one of them is designed to help the church and to help us be like Christ to other people.

WHAT ARE MY GIFTS?

Some people wonder why it's important to know what their spiritual gifts are. (We usually get more than one, by the way.) Maybe it will help if you put yourself in God's place for a minute. As the Giver, what would he want us to do with the gifts? When my son Steve was younger, we recognized he had enormous artistic talent that took a lot of different forms. He was interested in photography, so one year we spent some extra money and got him an expensive camera for Christmas. This camera didn't just point and shoot—the owner's manual was at least a few inches thick! The first thing Steve did was take out the camera and look it over. He was so excited about it, he spent the afternoon poring over the manual and learning about all the stuff the camera could do.

Over the next few months Steve took a lot of really bad pictures—and many great ones—as he practiced combining his natural talent and this new gift. And as he worked at developing his gift, he created some really cool stuff. Now how do you think we would have felt if Steve hadn't opened the gift? Or if he'd ignored it, letting it collect dust on the shelf? Or if he'd never bothered to learn how to use it properly? I'm pretty sure that God feels the same way about how we use our gifts from him. He has a purpose in giving them to us, and he delights in watching us receive them, develop them, and use them for that good purpose.

The tricky thing about discovering your gifts is that when they're undeveloped, they're often hard to recognize. There are tests you can take (I've included a really simple one here) and books you can read, but the best thing to do is to pray and pay attention. Notice the evidence in your life of what feels to you like a special ability and also what abilities others affirm in you. Our gifts can often clue us in as to the work God wants us to do.

One of the things you need to be really careful about is what I call "gift envy." It's easy to see another person doing something well and want that same ability for ourselves. I've seen lots of people really hurt themselves by wasting a bunch of energy pretending they have certain gifts instead of developing their true gifts.

Okay, look at each sentence and rate yourself according to the following key:

1—if the statement is almost never true of you
2—if it's rarely true
3—if it's sometimes true
4—if it's often true

1. I don't really need lots of attention; I just like to do what needs doing. _____
2. I like to help people learn. _____
3. I have a knack for saying things to people or doing things for them that makes them feel helped or healed. _____
4. I tend to give a lot of stuff away, including money. _____
5. People look to me for direction and follow my lead in things. _____
6. I feel great compassion for people who are suffering. _____
7. I seem to have insight and understanding into things that others struggle with. _____

8. There are times when God seems to reveal specific things to me about people, situations, or Scripture that are not possible for me to know on my own. _____
9. I seem to have extraordinary confidence in God. _____
10. I have a strong desire for people to be healed from physical, emotional, and spiritual sickness. _____
11. I have a strong sense of the presence of good and evil. _____
12. At times my prayers are uttered in a language I have never learned. _____
13. When others are praying in a foreign tongue, I can understand what they are saying even though the language is not familiar to me. _____
14. I have the ability to organize people and projects to accomplish goals. _____
15. I sometimes have a strong sense of something God wants to communicate to his people. _____
16. I like to do things I see need doing for people and my church. _____
17. I seem to have a knack for helping people understand things, either by explaining or showing them. _____
18. I tend to see the positive things in people—sometimes things they don't see in themselves. _____
19. I think one of the best things about making money is being able to give it to people who need it more than I do. _____
20. I love to rally people around a common purpose and get to work on it. _____
21. I desire to find ways to ease the distress of people who are struggling. _____
22. The Holy Spirit seems to give me insight into how to apply God's Word and leadings in specific situations. _____
23. Sometimes I sense that when I am praying, God answers with specific words, phrases, or images. _____
24. Even though sometimes I experience twinges of doubt, most of the time I have a certainty about the will and purposes of God. _____

25. When I've touched or prayed for people, they've experienced some type of healing. ____
26. I can often tell when the cause of a behavior or thought is coming from God or from some demonic source. ____
27. I sometimes pray in a language that seems like one only God and I know. ____
28. I can sometimes interpret another person's prayer language. ____
29. When God gives the church a vision or plan for something, I do well at knowing how to get that plan accomplished. ____
30. There are occasions during prayer when God seems to give me specific messages for the church or specific people. ____

Okay, now add your scores together for the following pairs of statements:

1 and 16 (A) ____
2 and 17 (B) ____
3 and 18 (C) ____
4 and 19 (D) ____
5 and 20 (E) ____
6 and 21 (F) ____
7 and 22 (G) ____
8 and 23 (H) ____
9 and 24 (I) ____
10 and 25 (J) ____
11 and 26 (K) ____
12 and 27 (L) ____
13 and 28 (M) ____
14 and 29 (N) ____
15 and 30 (O) ____

Once you've added these pairs of numbers together, go back and highlight or circle the pairs of statements that received the three highest scores. If more than three of the above pairings received the same score, read the following descriptions to help you identify the three that resonate with you the most.

If your highest score was A, you may have the gift of *serving*. People with this gift seem to have a special love for doing practical and helpful things for others.

If your highest score was B, you may have the gift of *teaching*. This doesn't necessarily mean you should be a schoolteacher, but people with this gift have the special ability to help others understand things and add to their knowledge.

If your highest score was C, you may have the gift of *encouragement*. This gift can be used in the form of words, actions, or tokens of affection—anything that gives another person a lift.

If your highest score was D, you may have the gift of *giving.* People with this gift have a naturally stronger desire than most people to give (including money).

If your highest score was E, you may have the gift of *leadership.* If people tend to follow you, and you have the ability to rally people around a task or vision, then you may have this gift.

If your highest score was F, you may have the gift of *mercy.* People with this gift can often feel a supernatural empathy or compassion for others who are hurting.

If your highest score was G, you may have the gift of *wisdom.* People with this gift report having a strong sense of knowing God's will about people and situations in ways that are consistent with the nature of God as found in Scripture.

If your highest score was H, you may have the gift of *knowledge.* God gives some people the ability to know things about others that are hidden from everyone else. This gift seems given for the purposes of healing and prayer.

If your highest score was I, you may have the gift of *faith.* This gift is the ability to believe God and his Word with great confidence. (Note: The gift of faith doesn't equal total absence of doubt at all times!)

If your highest score was J, you may have the gift of *healing.* This gift is the ability to bring a healing touch from God to others. It may be displayed through prayer, touch, or many other ways. God uses people with this gift to bring physical, emotional, and spiritual healing.

If your highest score was K, you may have the gift of *discernment.* This gift is the ability to detect the source of something as coming from God or from evil.

If your highest score was L, you may have the gift of *tongues.* This is a special prayer language that can be unintelligible but still meaningful to the person who is praying and others who have the gift of interpretation.

If your highest score was M, you may have the gift of *interpretation.* This is the ability to understand another person's prayer language.

If your highest score was N, you may have the gift of *administration.* Some people have a special ability to organize tasks through strategies, processes, or procedures that enable them to get the job done well.

If your highest score was O, you may have the gift of *prophecy.* God gives this gift to some of his people so they can clearly hear what he wants to tell his people specifically. Many times he wants people to pray about these things.

TEMPERAMENT

Have you ever wondered how you could be raised in the same home as your siblings and parents but end up so *different?* Or how you could be so like another person who was raised completely differently than you? I'm sure you've been told your whole life that you are unique—a complete original.

Your temperament is the inner wiring of your personality, the source of a lot of your behavior. Your temperament is what makes you basically shy or outgoing, neat or messy, a risk taker or steady and reliable. Your temperament is affected by your environment but not created by it.

Leaders need to understand people. As you lead, you will need to help people discover and maximize their strengths as well as understand and overcome their weaknesses. But the first step is to become a student of you. Thoroughly knowing yourself—the good and the not-so-good parts—is essential to being a fully integrated leader.

The idea of identifying (or "typing") temperaments isn't a new one. It goes back as far as the ancient Greeks—and maybe farther. Hippocrates noticed four major types of temperaments in people. His theory was that some people had an abundance of a particular body fluid, which influenced their behavior. He named the four temperaments after the fluids or humors he thought were the cause:

- Blood was associated with a temperament that was cheerful, warm, and pleasant, or sanguine.
- Phlegm was thought to produce a calm, slow-moving, or phlegmatic temperament.
- Black bile supposedly resulted in a sad, depressed, or melancholic temperament.
- Yellow bile was responsible for a choleric temperament, which meant the person was hot tempered or quick to react.

It's a pretty gross idea, which scientists have since proven untrue, but the four groupings Hippocrates identified have nevertheless stood the test of time. You can find the same theory in many of the temperament-typing systems that are commonly used today.

Understanding temperaments is too complex to explore fully in this chapter and too important for just a quickie quiz. However, the Take It Deeper section of this chapter will give you some direction for discovering your temperament. And while you may be tempted to skip it—DON'T!

For now you can begin thinking about some things that will help you in that process. One of the things your temperament determines is your strengths and weaknesses. It's important to understand that most of the time our strengths and weaknesses are two sides of the same coin. When you push too hard into one of them, you end up on the other side. For example, one of my strengths is communicating with people. It's a good trait, but when I overdo it by being too talkative, my strength becomes a weakness. Being realistic about these things is incredibly important as you develop your leadership abilities, integrating who you are with what you do.

Take some time to think and pray about the traits present in you when you're at your best. You may come up with words such as *organized, decisive, patient, loyal, inspirational, friendly,* or *creative.*

Strengths:

________ ________ ________ ________ ________

Next try to come up with five words to describe those strengths (one descriptive word for each strength) and write them on the appropriate lines below.

Strength Descriptions:

________ ________ ________ ________ ________

Now write words to describe the exact opposites of your strengths. These represent the other side of the coin I referred to earlier. If you are finding it difficult to think of a description for a particular strength, try starting with a weakness instead. Once you have that word in mind, come up with its opposite to discover the corresponding strength.

Opposites:

________ ________ ________ ________ ________

YOUR VALUES

Your values are the principles you live by or the things that are important to you. When you have decisions to make, your values often guide your decision-making. Think of it like this: When you get to the end of your life, what do you want people to say about you? For what causes did you take a stand? Leaders who lead from an integrated heart know their values and incorporate them into their daily lives.

Grab your journal again. Make a list of all the important things in your life. When you're finished, look through the list and pick the five that are the most important to you. List them here along with a sentence to define what each value means to you.

Example:
FAMILY—Nurturing and protecting the relationships I have with the people with whom I will share life from cardle to grave.

1.

2.

3.

4.

5.

"You can't lead others until you've first led yourself through a struggle with your values."

—JAMES M. KOUZES AND BARRY Z. POSNER, THE LEADERSHIP CHALLENGE

YOUR THINKING STYLE

Along with giving you a particular temperament, God has hardwired you with a thinking style. Everyone seems to fall somewhere between concrete thinker and abstract thinker.

Concrete thinkers tend to be pretty black-and-white about things. They think in absolutes, using words such as *always* and *never* frequently. Concrete thinkers prefer things clear, defined, and orderly. They generally aren't huge risk takers and are pretty comfortable with routines. They're the ones who sometimes say, "Just tell me what to do, and I'll do it."

On the other end of the spectrum are abstract thinkers. They live in the land of ideas and theories. They are usually creative, spontaneous, and highly changeable. They take huge risks and get bored very quickly if they have to do the same thing for too long.

Most people fall somewhere in the middle. The thing to remember is that, like temperaments, there isn't any one thinking style that's best. We need them all. Imagine a team of people who have a project to finish. First someone needs to have an overall vision for the project. Then another person needs to figure out how to turn the dream into reality—to come up with a strategy. Someone else needs to see the big picture and put things in motion. The project also needs a manager-type person, someone who can see and corral the details of the smaller tasks and organize the people who are doing those tasks and keep the momentum going. And of course the team will need people who like to do those tasks. These people are happiest when they have a specific job that they know how to do and are released to do it.

This team of people represents the continuum of thinking styles from abstract to concrete. Can you see why it's important to know your own thinking style? If you are a leader who is more of a dreamer, but you put yourself in a managerial role, you'll likely end up frustrated—and you'll frustrate other people, too.

Leaders who lead from an integrated heart know what kinds of thinkers they are so they can spend most of their time in roles where they'll be able to give their best and—maybe more importantly—so they can surround themselves with people who think differently from them.

Look at the following diagram of the continuum of thinking styles. Where do you fit?

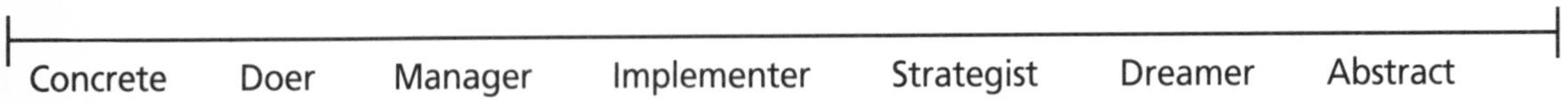

Concrete Doer Manager Implementer Strategist Dreamer Abstract

TAKE IT DEEPER

Mark your spot on the path and then write a few sentences to describe the evidence you have to support your choice.

ADDITIONAL RESOURCES

Discovering your temperament is way more complicated than those little magazine quizzes make it seem. Many helpful tools have been developed over the years to help people understand their temperaments. Check out at least two of the resources on this list. There are lots more, but these should give you a good start.

Books—

What You Do Best in the Body of Christ by Bruce Bugbee
Spirit-Controlled Temperament by Tim LaHaye
Personality Plus: How to Understand Others by Understanding Yourself by Florence Littauer
LifeKeys: Discovering Who You Are, Why You're Here, What You Do Best by Jane A.G. Kise, David Stark, and Sandra Krebs Hirsh
Please Understand Me: Character and Temperament Types by David Keirsey and Marilyn Bates

You may also want to check out—

SoulTypes by Robert Norton and Richard Southern (talks about discovering your spiritual DNA)
Certain Trumpets: The Nature of Leadership by Garry Wills (about different leadership styles)
Sacred Pathways by Gary Thomas (I strongly recommend you check out this one. The author claims people are hard-wired to experience or commune with God in different ways. Cool stuff!)

Online—

www.advisorteam.com/user/ktsintro.asp (temperament sorter)
www.mintools.com/personality.htm
www.online-asap.com/survey-Chesapeake.pdf

JOURNALING SNAPSHOTS

DAY 1

Read James 3:1-12. It doesn't matter how much talent, ability, or intelligence a leader has. If a leader is unable to control his tongue, it's all for nothing. In your journal today reflect on how you've used your tongue either to build others up or to tear them down. If appropriate, write out a confession to God and ask for his help in making it right with anyone you may have hurt.

DAY 2

Read 1 Chronicles 16:8-12 out loud. There are nine commands in this passage. In order for a leader to be led by God, first she needs to obey him. We sometimes wonder about God's will for our lives. I've found that I often discover the answer to this question when I obey the things he wants me to do—things that are clearly shown in his Word. In your journal write out each verse of this passage, one on each line, and then write your own response after it.

Example: *VERSE 8: Give thanks to the Lord—I'm thankful for my friends, family, and church.*

DAY 3

Read Proverbs 11:25; Acts 3:19; 1 Corinthians 16:18; and Philemon 7 and 20. What word do these passages have in common? In your Bible underline every occurrence of this word in these four passages. God knows the challenges of leadership are great, and he desires to give us times of refreshment. How does God refresh you? For me it's often during times spent with good friends—especially when there's a lot of laughter! Thank God specifically for the recent times of refreshment he's given to you.

DAY 4

Read Micah 6:8. Think about the things God requires of you. What does it look like for a leader to be just, merciful, and humble? In your journal today reflect on what this passage means to you.

DAY 5

Read 2 Corinthians 3:4-6. Here is a reminder of where your strengths really come from. Confess the ways you've wrongly relied on your own strengths.

■ CHAPTER THREE

THE PRAYING LEADER

Think about this for a minute: God gave you the spiritual gift to lead, a temperament he specifically created for you, and specific work he intended you to do—so why step out and lead without him? That's like an athlete playing an entire game without talking to the coach. How would the player know what strategy the coach had in mind? Or it would be like a server in a restaurant trying to tell the cook what to prepare without first consulting the customer. Is it possible to do? Of course. Is it a good idea? Not at all.

I once knew a guy who was a natural leader. He had all the gifts, passion, and abilities to lead well. One day he came to me in frustration over a project he was trying to lead at his school. It seemed as if nothing was working out right, and he was ready to quit. I asked him how much he'd prayed about it. His response? "Well, I don't really pray much. Praying is boring. I'm just not into it. I'm too ADHD. Hey, God gets that. He made me this way!"

What this guy *didn't* get was that in order to lead from an integrated heart, part of what needs integrating is the voice of

God. Kingdom leaders aren't praying leaders because they're *supposed* to pray; they're praying leaders because they can't help it. They just can't lead without talking to God about it first.

Are you one of those leaders who fears what God may reveal to you in prayer? Hey, it's not easy! In one conversation with God, David admits, "Your servant has found courage to pray to you" (1 Chronicles 17:25). Even King David had to find the courage to pray. By the way, do you know how David found that courage? He paid attention to what God was doing, and when David recognized that God was revealing the work he wanted David to do, it gave him the courage he needed to pray. How cool is that?

This chapter is about beginning the process of integrating your conversations with God into your heart and into your leadership. Please keep in mind that this is a process. Don't get discouraged if this feels like hard stuff at first. Sometimes things such as prayer feel harder than they need to because we try too hard to do it the way everyone else seems to be doing it. Your prayer life is *your* conversation with God. It should happen the way God created it to happen with *you*. As we get started, let's check out a couple of cool things that happen when we pray, and then you can practice praying in some new ways.

THE CONVERSATION IS THE RELATIONSHIP

One of the most important relationships in my life is with my good friend Shelley. Something I love about my friendship with her is how we can talk about anything. When wonderful things happen in my life, I can't wait to tell her about them. When tragedy or difficulties come, she hears about them. Sometimes we both get pretty busy with life, and we can go a week or two without really connecting. Other times we get into periods where our lives seem to intersect at points, and we sort of do the basic maintenance thing—I don't really know what's in her heart, and she doesn't know what's in mine. In those times we feel as if we've maintained the relationship because we've touched base for at least a few minutes, and it's fine. Fine, that is, if we don't try to build our friendship on those brief encounters alone. It's the time we've invested in the *deeper* conversations—the kind that can't happen in quick, snatched moments—that forms the essential fabric of our friendship.

That's what our prayer life can be like as well. The brief connections—"God, I need you. God bless my friends. Help me with my homework. Thank you for this day"—can lead us to believe that we're really praying, we're doing our duty, we're connecting with God. But in reality we're just barely maintaining our end of the relationship.

Conversation in a friendship doesn't just maintain the sense of connection between two people. The language of a relationship does the work of shaping and refining it. Sometimes Shelley is like a mirror for me. She offers a truer reflection of myself than the one I see every morning while I brush my teeth. She reflects back to me who I really am. When she asks me for advice, she's telling me I'm trustworthy. When she laughs with me, she tells me I'm fun to be with—at least sometimes. When she cries with me, she tells me I'm important and that my struggles are real. She encourages me when I do certain things well, so I know where I should invest my energy and time. Because she is my friend and she loves me, she tells me the hard things, too—not just that I have a piece of spinach in my teeth (which she *would* tell me), but also when I need to adjust my attitude, priorities, or response to a situation.

A few years ago I was telling Shelley about a conversation I'd had with a person who was really frustrating me. He'd asked me to do something I thought was ridiculous. So I was reliving the conversation for her, including the stunningly sarcastic remark that had finally shut that person down. I sadly admit to you that I was pretty proud of myself as I told the tale. I thought I was witty and brilliant for coming up with just the right stinging comeback for this idiotic proposal. As I finished my account and internally sighed with satisfaction,

Shelley looked at me and quietly said, "I wouldn't like you very much if you said that to me."

I sat in stunned silence for a few moments as I absorbed her words. This quiet, truth-filled reply was the very thing I needed to hear to understand this fact: I am not always kind. I use sarcasm as a deadly weapon to assassinate those who irritate me. I realized I would never speak to Shelley that way—so why would I do it to someone else? I knew I needed to change.

Communicating with God is a lot like that. When I tell him about the things that are on my heart—things I long for, things I struggle with, things I need—he reflects them back to me. He teaches, encourages, and disciplines me. He corrects me. Because God knows me so well, he can tell me things I don't know or haven't seen in myself. Just as with my friend Shelley, my conversation with God is my relationship with him.

What are the things God might be telling you right now?

How have your times of prayer encouraged you or taught you new things?

PRAYER—THE PRIDE BUSTER

The greatest enemy of every leader is pride. As the old saying goes, "Power corrupts." It's so easy to fall into a pattern of self-reliance and independence. When people look to you as if you have all the answers, you begin to believe it. When you get to make the decisions, you start to believe no one else can. You have success in your leadership endeavor, and people praise you. Pretty soon you can become addicted to that praise. One of the leaders in my life once said to me, "Don't forget that you cannot trust me. I will fail you. Only trust the Spirit of God in me." I know he is a praying leader. I can follow him with confidence because he often speaks of the things God teaches him and directs him to in prayer, and he prays often with the people he leads. When people speak of him, *humility* is a word often used.

If you've been drifting a little during all of this reading, sit up for a minute and take a deep breath. I want you to really get this next part—God does not want you to be a praying leader just for your own benefit! God does not direct us to pray just so we can receive godly direction for our own lives or so we can have a close and intimate relationship with him, although those things do occur and are important. There's more! We are to be praying leaders for the sake of our *communities*—those we live with, serve with, lead, and follow. When we pray, God moves in ways that affect others besides you.

Nehemiah is one of the great leaders of the Bible. He fasts, prays, and confesses not only his own sins, but also the sins of his entire nation (Nehemiah 1)! God hears his prayers and uses Nehemiah to lead the efforts to rebuild the temple of Jerusalem and bring Israel back into fellowship with God. In 2 Chronicles 30 we see how King Hezekiah cries out in prayer on behalf of his people and how the Lord "heard Hezekiah and healed the people" (verse 20). And Acts 10 and 11 show us how two important leaders, Peter and Cornelius, a Jew and a Gentile, are praying leaders who hear things from God and obediently act on them, setting the stage for the birth of the church and the acceptance of the Gentiles into the kingdom of

God. Both of these leaders needed to be praying and listening because if only one of them had been, the story would have ended very differently. Often when we hear things from God in prayer, God is giving us just a piece of what he is saying to his people. When leaders pray, they become part of the bigger conversation God wants to have with his people.

I once spent three days fasting and praying. After doing so, I felt an urge to call a man I had confidence in for his spiritual guidance. He lived quite a distance away, but I called and asked him if he would come and pray for me. He came, and I was all ready to place myself before him and let him minister to me.

Instead he sat down in front of me and started confessing his sins. I thought, I'm supposed to do that to you. After he finished, and I had prayed forgiveness for him, he said, "Now do you still want me to pray for you?"

All of a sudden I realized his discernment. He knew I had thought of him as a spiritual giant who was going to set me right. Only then did he place his hands on me and pray for me.

—RICHARD FOSTER, "SPIRITUALITY AND SERVING GOD" (LEADERSHIP JOURNAL, JANUARY 2002)

Jesus is, of course, our ultimate model of a praying leader. Luke 5:16 says, "Jesus often withdrew to lonely places and prayed." He spent 40 days fasting and praying before he even began his ministry. Prayer shaped his decisions. For example, he prayed all night before he chose his 12 disciples (Luke 6:12-16). Prayer determined the direction of his ministry (Mark 1:35-38). He taught us how to pray (Matthew 6:9-13), and he prayed for us (John 17). In fact, he could do *nothing* without God revealing it to him in prayer (John 5:19).

One of the most dangerous things a leader can do is try to make plans apart from God's direction: "The Lord foils the plans of the nations; he thwarts the purposes of the peoples. But the plans of the Lord stand firm forever, the purposes of his heart through all generations" (Psalm 33:10-11).

Scripture repeatedly shows us in great detail not only the need for leaders to pray, but also the consequences that befall leaders who fail to pray. Check out 1 Samuel 12:6-23. Samuel calls it a sin to fail to pray for those we lead. Remember Saul? Samuel anoints him king before he anoints David. God chooses Saul to be king of Israel, but what happens to him? Look at 1 Chronicles 10:13-14, "Saul died because he was unfaithful to the Lord...and did not inquire of the Lord." In the worldly sense Saul was a great leader. He had a great military mind. He had the experience and the skills to be a great king. But ultimately, he was a failure because he wanted to rely on those skills and his own plans instead of asking God what his will was for Israel. Ouch!

As you continue your study on leadership, don't ever forget that you can possess every skill necessary to be a great leader, but unless you also allow the living God to shape the integrity of your heart, it will all come to nothing.

TAKE IT DEEPER

NEW WAYS TO PRAY

There are so many different ways to pray! Read through this list of prayer exercises, pick two that appeal to you, and plan to try them this week.

1. Rent a movie, listen to a CD, or read a section of a good novel. As you experience it, pay close attention to your thoughts and feelings and jot them down in a notebook—even if they seem insignificant at the time. These may be observations about characters—things that provoke awareness of yourself and your own behaviors. Use these notes as a basis for a prayer time. Your sensory experience may cause you to think of something you've done wrong that you need to fix, a relationship that needs repairing, an aspect of your character that needs attention, or a person who needs prayer. After you've jotted down whatever your experience brings to mind—all the assorted thoughts and impressions—look them over, try to discern a common theme, and then use that as a springboard for your prayer time.

2. Get a copy of the prayer list insert in your church's Sunday bulletin. Pray for each ill and needy person on the list and ask God where he wants you to enter into his work in those people's lives. He may lead you to send a card to let someone know you are praying for her, to visit someone in the hospital, or even to perform a service of some kind. Keep listening for ways, and he will guide you.

3. For this exercise you will need your Bible and your journal. Take a moment and ask God to speak to you through his Word. Repeat the words, "Speak, Lord, your servant is listening," several times. Read Isaiah 30:18 out loud: "Yet the Lord longs to be gracious to you; he rises to show you compassion. For the Lord is a God of justice. Blessed are all who wait for him!" Read it again silently at least once and perhaps a few more times until one word or phrase

■■■

jumps out at you. Record that word or phrase in your journal. Read the verse again, this time asking, "What are you saying to me through this word, Lord?" Record whatever comes to your mind. Now read it out loud again. Ask God what he wants you to do with what he is telling you. Again record what you hear.

4. Using a concordance, look up at least five passages of Scripture that speak of God's love. Write about them in your journal. Ask God to speak to you about all the ways he has shown his love for you in your life. Be silent for a while and allow the memories and mental pictures to flow. Spend some time recording them in your journal and then pray again, reflecting back to God all the ways you love him.

5. Select a passage of Scripture to study. (Don't spend too much time selecting it. It can be randomly chosen.) Pray for a few moments and ask God not only to bring new revelation and understanding to you as you study the passage, but also to teach you and change you as a result of your study. Read through the passage slowly, looking up every cross-reference your Bible lists. (These are often found in the margin or in the notes at the bottom of the page.) When reading a story, try to visualize what is happening. Circle any words or phrases that are repeated. Continue to pray for understanding as you read and study. Record in your journal anything you learn or understand from reading this passage.

6. Take your Bible and a notebook outside with you. (Keep a separate journal or notebook that you use just for this purpose.) Go to the beach, the woods, a field, a river—wherever you enjoy being outdoors. Focus on something in your surroundings—a rock, a flower, rushing water, whatever you can observe from where you are sitting. Read some passages of Scripture and then spend a few minutes just being quiet. Record any impressions or thoughts you have. Anything that goes through your mind—write it down. Take breaks

and refocus your attention on your surroundings every few minutes but keep jotting things down as they come. When you're ready, look through your list and circle or underline the things you feel you can pray for. Sometimes being in a natural environment feeds you so deeply that you just want to give thanks to God. If the things you see remind you of aspects of God's character, write them down and pray those things to him.

7. Divide a notebook into several sections and label each one to fit you and your interests or the areas of your life that you want to pray for—friends, family, school, work, personal. Within each general section write a different name or title at the top of every other page. You may find it helpful to put small pictures or other items on each person's page to serve as a visual reminder of them. (One way to do this is to ask the people you are praying for to trace their handprints onto pages in your prayer journal.) Then use these pages to record the needs and prayer requests of the people or situations you've included in your notebook. You can use one page to record prayer requests and the other pages to record answers. Or you can divide pages in half—whatever style works for you. During your prayer time flip through the pages of the notebook and use it as a guide. You don't need to add new things to each section every time you pray. In fact, you may feel most comfortable praying for the same things each day until you can see clear answers.

Be not anxious because of your helplessness. Above all, do not let it prevent you from praying. Helplessness is the real secret and the impelling power of prayer. You should therefore rather try to thank God for the feeling of helplessness, which He has given to you.

It is one of the greatest gifts that God can impart to us. For it is only when we are helpless that we open our hearts to Jesus and let Him help us in our distress, according to His grace and mercy.

—O. HALLESBY, **PRAYER**

JOURNALING SNAPSHOTS

DAY 1

Read Jeremiah 9:23-24; Matthew 11:29; and Philippians 3:8,10. Spend some time today thinking about Jesus and who he is. Write a response to him about what that means to you.

DAY 2

Read Philippians 3:7-8. Write to Jesus today and tell him about all the things you're willing to count as nothing compared to knowing him and seeing his glory.

DAY 3

Read 1 Chronicles 21:11-27 and 2 Samuel 24:18-25. Think through all of the things you sacrifice for Jesus. Have they cost you anything? Write in your journal about the cost of those sacrifices.

DAY 4

Read Exodus 15:13; Psalm 143:8; and Romans 5:5-8. Pray these verses in your journal with your family, friends, and community in mind.

DAY 5

Read Matthew 10:42. Who needs a cup of cold water from you today? Write about it in your journal, asking God to bring faces and ideas to your mind.

■ CHAPTER FOUR

THE SERVING LEADER

Lead•er \'lē-dər \ *n* one in charge or command of others

Ser•vant \'sər-vənt \ *n* one who expresses submission, recognizance, or debt to another person

Par•a•dox \'par-ə-,däks \ *n* a seemingly contradictory statement that may nonetheless be true

The idea of servant leadership is really the ultimate paradox. It didn't make sense to the disciples when Jesus explained it to them, and it doesn't make sense to us now. The leader is supposed to be the one in charge—the master, so to speak. And the servant is the one who serves the master—right?

Not according to Jesus. The disciples have pegged Jesus as the next king; and he is—only he is a different kind of king than they've imagined. When they begin to argue about who is the most powerful among them, Jesus turns their suppositions upside down: "Whoever wants to become great among you must be your servant, and whoever wants to be first must be slave of all. For even the Son of Man did not come to be served, but to serve, and to give his life as a ransom for many" (Mark 10:43-45).

Imagine how blown away those disciples must have been. Imagine what they must have been thinking, *This guy is gonna be the next king, and I'm right in line to be his number one guy! Sweet!* Instead Jesus tells them they have to be like servants.

Truthfully, we're not any different from the disciples. We think of a servant as someone who's unable to think for himself and who only does the bidding of his master. We also think of a leader as someone who does the choosing for whomever he leads. Then how can someone be both a servant and a leader at the same time? As my friend Denny Gunderson says, "Servant leadership is so radical, so heavenly, we have missed it." In fact, servant leadership is so radical that it really defies everything our culture teaches us about leadership. It was true in Jesus' day, and it's true today.

Servant leadership is a choice. It doesn't matter what your spiritual gifts are, whether or not you are popular, or even whether or not you like to serve others. Every leader in the kingdom of God is expected to lead by serving.

But let's be honest—it's not easy. We don't always *feel* like serving. To tell the truth, sometimes we really *like* being served. Being a servant leader doesn't mean others will never serve you. In fact, we are *commanded* to serve one another. So an important part of being a servant leader is modeling humility as you graciously accept another person's service to you.

SERVANT LEADERSHIP IN THE BIBLE

How then do we become servant leaders? How do we choose to be the kind of leader Jesus was when our culture and our fleshly desires tell us otherwise? Let's explore this together.

We will begin by reading a very cool book in the Bible that you may not have noticed before—the book of Ruth. And even if you have read it recently, grab your Bible and dig in anyway. It's a really short book, so make sure you read the whole thing. (C'mon! It won't take long!)

What are your initial impressions of the book of Ruth?

What things struck you?

As we absorb this beautiful story of love, commitment, and redemption, God gives us glimpses into the many ways we serve one another. Do you think serving only means doing stuff for others? You're in for a big surprise! There are tons of ways to serve others, and the characters in this awesome little book model several different ways of doing it. Let's look at a few of them.

On the surface Naomi is an ordinary woman. She isn't rich or famous in any way, but she does have a few things going for her. She couldn't give riches to her sons' wives, but she generously gives them what she does have.

Look back at the story and see if you can pick out the ways Naomi serves by giving from these resources.

Authority:

Wisdom:

Experience:

Ruth also sacrificially serves in many ways. For a young girl whose husband has just died and left her living in a foreign culture with his mother, she steps up pretty well.

As you read through the text, jot down a few notes about how Ruth serves by giving of these resources.

Time:

Energy:

Youth:

Strength:

The other important character in this story is pretty amazing, too. Boaz doesn't even know Naomi and Ruth when the story begins, but he serves them both quite selflessly.

Did you notice how Boaz gives away the following resources? Look for these and note anything else you find.

Wealth:

Position:

Other:

The common theme between these three people's acts of servanthood is their willingness to give sacrificially of whatever resources they possess. Do you want to understand servant leadership? Do you want to really get it? Then you have to understand the difference between servant leadership and acts of service. Performing acts of service, while certainly an important type of servanthood, does not even begin to define the essence of what Jesus really calls leaders to do. He asks us to be servants who lead, not just leaders who serve. Read that sentence again: He asks us to be servants who lead, not just leaders who serve. When Jesus tells the disciples that the one who wants to become great among them must "be your servant," he is referring more to the being than the doing of the leader.

"True heroism is remarkably sober, very undramatic. It is not the urge to surpass all others at whatever cost, but the urge to serve others at whatever cost."
—ARTHUR ASHE, TENNIS CHAMPION AND AIDS VICTIM, WWW.THINKEXIST.COM

SERVANT LEADERSHIP TODAY

Okay, so now what? Are there real steps you can take to become a serving leader? Let's take a look at some of the things we've learned from Ruth, Naomi, and Boaz and see how we can put them into practice.

STEP ONE: ATTITUDE

During one season of the NBC drama *The West Wing*, a character named Ainsley Hayes is a staunch Republican lawyer who is hired to work in the legal department of a Democrat-controlled White House. After a rocky start to her new job, she tells the chief of staff that she's thinking about quitting. After she unloads all the grief she's endured and essentially says, "They hate me, I can't take it anymore, and I'm quitting," the chief of staff smiles at her and says in a stern-yet-gentle voice, "Ainsley, you are here to serve the president." In other words, her presence in the White House was solely to serve one person—the President of the United States. If the other staffers weren't happy about her being there, too bad! Her focus needed to be on *giving the best she could give to the one she was there to serve.*

It's the same with you. Your focus can't be on the reactions of those around you; you must focus on the one you are ultimately serving—Jesus. When we serve him by serving those we lead, we may not get the recognition, thanks, or credit we may think we deserve. But it doesn't matter. In fact, it is better for us if we don't receive it.

Think about a time when you served another person in some way.

What was your true motive?

What prompted you to do it?

When we serve others out of anything but a sincere motive of servanthood, it becomes *manipulation*—a mere stepping-stone to gain favor, status, or a tangible reward. Has someone ever done something for you, and all the while you knew she was really just trying to get you to like her or to do something for her in return? When the motives are wrong, the person on the receiving end often feels used instead of served. As you read Ruth's story, did you notice how each character has the attitude of a servant? In fact, Ruth refers to herself as a servant, and Boaz responds that the Lord will repay her for what she has done. When Ruth chooses to remain loyal to her mother-in-law and to do whatever it takes to provide for her, she is truly serving God.

STEP TWO: RELINQUISHMENT

Relinquishing something means surrendering it, totally giving it up. In order to truly serve others, we have to relinquish things. First and foremost, true servanthood requires you to let go of your *pride*. Thinking of yourself as better than the person you are serving gets you into trouble. If there are things about others that prevent you from serving them in some way—their clothes, who they hang with, their annoying habits—then you'd better examine your pride level. If you find yourself worrying about what others might think if they find out you serve a particular person, check that pride. Or if you make sure someone else notices your act of service—then you've also got a problem.

Pride is the biggest killer of a servant attitude. The two cannot coexist. Notice I wrote "servant *attitude.*" A prideful person can certainly perform acts of service, and many do. However, prideful people process their decisions through the filter of self first, not through the filter of what others might need.

Author Dan Webster calls this the "disease of me." It's a good name for it because that's exactly what pride is—a disease, and it's a fatal one. On the contrary, did you notice Ruth's attitude? What a great example of a servant who has surrendered her pride. Before her husband died, Ruth probably had a comfortable lifestyle. But now she assumes a position lower than a servant girl's in order to provide food for her mother-in-law. And how about Naomi? She is probably used to taking care of her own family, so it must be hard for Naomi to allow her daughter-in-law to go out to the fields each day and do the backbreaking work of gathering grain from the harvest leftovers.

"What is so ridiculous about the idea that a person could be cleaning toilets one day and have an 'important ministry' the next—or vice versa? Preparation for ruling and reigning with Christ does not begin with ruling and reigning. It begins and ends with service... The leader who wants to do only big things for God reveals the true nature of his motives."

—DENNY GUNDERSON, **THE LEADERSHIP PARADOX**

That brings us to another place of relinquishment. A servant leader must also surrender position. When Jesus puts on a towel and begins washing the feet of the disciples in John 13, he shatters their expectations of the kind of king he is going to be. Now read John 13:8.

How does Peter react when he realizes Jesus is about to perform the most basic act of servanthood for him?

A few years ago I began taking a weightlifting class. On the first day Deb, the instructor, announced that everyone was required to do chin-ups. Having not done a chin-up since about fifth grade, I began to look for somewhere to hide. One by one Deb began calling people over to the chin-up bars as the rest of us worked out on the various machines. I kept my eye on her and successfully dodged her for almost the entire hour. However, the fateful moment finally arrived when the last person finished, and I accidentally made eye contact with Deb.

She called me over. I gulped and then drew a deep breath. Since I couldn't think of a way to get out of doing it without embarrassing myself worse than my impending failure on the chin-up bar, I walked over to her. I figured I might as well get it over with, so I stood up on the chair and let my body drop down as I held onto that bar for dear life. I tried to hoist myself up. My heart stopped. It was worse than I thought—my elbows were locked and I could not move. I was mortified. I'd spent an hour listening to the others count off, "One… two…three…four…" and now I wasn't even going to make it to one!

Deb interrupted my rising panic attack: "Whoa—wait a minute. Let me help you." She moved in closer to me and bent her knees. She placed my feet on her thighs and grabbed hold of my ankles. "Now try it."

One...two...three...! Slowly but surely, I pulled out three chin-ups. It was the weirdest thing. I wasn't pushing on her legs, and she wasn't pushing me. But somehow my weight was distributed differently, and I had the support I needed to get the job done. What a beautiful picture of servant leadership. Instead of standing back and watching to see how I was going to do, Deb positioned herself beneath me—supporting, encouraging, and leading me to do what I needed to do. She didn't do the chin-ups for me, she didn't get frustrated when I couldn't do them on my own, and she didn't push me. She got right in there and put my dirty old tennis shoes on her legs and led me through it. When I think of leadership, this is often the visual image I get—the leader in a bent, humble position beneath another, giving him the strength, support, and guidance to do what he needs to do.

"Angels can fly because they can take themselves lightly."
—G.K. CHESTERTON, **ORTHODOXY**

When you think of leadership, do you think of it as a position or an opportunity to serve?

Now, for all its failings and its perversions over the last 2,000 years—and as much as every exponent of this faith has attempted to dodge this idea—it is unarguably the central tenet of Christianity: that everybody is equal in God's eyes. So you cannot, as a Christian, walk away from Africa. America will be judged by God if, in its plenty, it crosses the road from 23 million people suffering from HIV, the leprosy of the day.

What's up on trial here is Christianity itself. You cannot walk away from this and call yourself a Christian and sit in power. Distance does not decide who is your brother and who is not.
—BONO, IN AN INTERVIEW WITH ANTHONY DECURTIS (WWW.BELIEFNET.COM, FEBRUARY 2001)

In the Trenches: Focus on U2's Bono

You probably know Bono as the lead singer of the band U2. Since the early 1980s, U2 has created some of the best rock music around. What you may not know is that Bono is perhaps most passionate about his work for Africa. He is one of the founders of a group called DATA, which stands for "Debt, Aid and Trade for Africa." Bono's passion for Africa began in 1985 when he became involved with Band Aid and Live Aid to raise money for the starving people living on that continent. But instead of just playing the gig and moving on, Bono and his wife actually traveled to Africa and worked in Ethiopian orphanages for six weeks. Since then he has traveled to Africa many times. He spends much of his time and money raising funds and awareness about the terrible crises of the AIDS epidemic and widespread poverty there. While he has talked about his Christian faith in different ways over the years, Bono has consistently acted out his faith more than he's talked about it. There is no doubt Bono is a serving leader.

STEP THREE: COMMITMENT

Being a servant leader requires an attitude of *commitment.* To me the commitment of a servant leader means being willing to do what is necessary *and going the extra mile.*

In Jesus' day there was a law that said if a Roman citizen asked someone to carry his burden, then that person was required to carry it for one mile. Remember, everyone walked everywhere in those days. Roman roads were crowded with people carrying their goods back and forth to the marketplace and women carrying heavy water jugs back and forth to the wells. If you were a Jew, it didn't matter if your arms were full. If a Roman citizen asked you to, you were required by law to set down your own burden, pick up the burden of the Roman, and carry it for the next mile. Look what Jesus has to say about it: "If someone forces you to go one mile, go with him two miles" (Matthew 5:41).

This is where we get our phrase "go the extra mile." Jesus didn't attack this unfair law. He told us to do it—*and then some.* He wants us to be "and then some" servants. Ruth could have said to Naomi, "Hey, I'll stick around until you're back on your feet. We'll get you set up somewhere, and then I'll go live my life." But she doesn't. She makes this radical statement: "Where you go I will go, and where you stay I will stay. Your people will be my people and your God my God" (Ruth 1:16). Whoa! She commits to serve Naomi in a new land with a new culture and a new religion. But she isn't finished. "Where you die I will die, and there I will be buried. May the Lord deal with me, be it ever so severely, if anything but death separates you and me" (Ruth 1:17). Now that's commitment! Ruth is saying to Naomi, "I'll give you everything I have, and then *I'll go an extra mile.*"

A few times a year I put together some big events that involve a lot of planning. One was a dinner for about 75 people, and I had asked several of our student leaders to help serve the food. After the meal I was saying goodbye to the last of the guests when I realized I'd completely forgotten to organize a cleanup team. (Duh!) My heart sank as I saw I was the only person left in the building, and I would probably be there for another hour or two cleaning the kitchen and putting away all the tables. But when I walked into the kitchen—surprise! It was spotless. All the work had already been done. Then I went into the room where we'd eaten and discovered the same thing—clean. There was nothing left to be done except turn off the lights. Those student leaders had done what I'd asked them to do—and then some. In that moment my respect and admiration—not to mention pure gratitude—for those students shot through the roof. In the months that followed, when things came up that needed solid leadership, I thought of those students first. They had demonstrated to me *rock-solid commitment* by going the extra mile, and as a direct result my trust in them as leaders increased quite a bit that night.

"It is too small a thing for you to be my servant to restore the tribes of Jacob and bring back those of Israel I have kept. I will also make you a light for the Gentiles, that you may bring my salvation to the ends of the earth."

—ISAIAH 49:6

When is the last time someone did something for you—and then some?

Is there any area in your life that God may be asking you to serve in an "and then some" way?

"The beginning and end of all Christian leadership is to give your life for others."
—HENRI NOUWEN, **THE WOUNDED HEALER**

STEP FOUR: SACRIFICE

Sacrifice. Ouch. No one really likes to think about sacrifice. After all, to sacrifice means to give up something of value, to pay the price. To serve others will cost us something, and we need to be willing to pay.

Many years ago I heard this impressive story. "Susan" spent a summer in Amsterdam with a group of college students. They were on an evangelistic mission, and their goal was to convert the drug addicts and prostitutes who lived in the "red light district," an area in the center of Amsterdam where pretty much everything is legal. Prostitutes, sex shops, "coffee shops" that sell drugs, and drug houses are everywhere. It's one of the darkest places in the world.

This team spent the summer walking through the district, passing out tracts, and trying to talk to people about Jesus. All except Susan. When the team went out to distribute their reading material, Susan left hers behind. Instead she went to a store and bought several cases of bottled water and passed the bottles out to the drug addicts lying on the hot streets. She cleaned prostitutes' apartments.

As the team debriefed together at the end of the summer, they counted the conversions they'd seen. The teams had passed out thousands of tracts and had talked to hundreds of people, but there had been only one conversion. Susan, on the other hand, counted more than 50 conversions as a result of her efforts that summer. Staggered, the team asked her what she had done. Susan simply replied, "Don't tell them Jesus loves them unless you are ready to love them, too." Susan paid the necessary price to win those people to Christ, and that love cost her plenty. She truly walked "through the dust" to lead those people to salvation in Christ.

Are you willing to risk the loss of friendships, reputation, time, financial security, even your very life, to answer the call of leadership?

What sacrifices might God be asking you to make right now?

A couple of years ago I went on a mission trip to Chicago. We were out on the streets doing some street evangelism. I was in a group with four other people I met on the trip. We were walking around, trying to find people to talk to, when we saw this homeless guy. He asked us for some food.

We knew there was a box of extra lunches in the van, but we didn't feel like going all the way back to get them. We gave him a couple bucks and walked away. Later we found out that another group had encountered the same guy and had gone back to get the lunches for him.

They ended up talking to him for a long time about Jesus. We missed such a great opportunity to really help someone just because we felt too tired and hot to walk to the van to get a guy some lunch.

—RACHEL REYBURN, AGE 16

STEP FIVE: DISCERNMENT

A lesson on servanthood would not be complete without a discussion on the topic of discernment. It's important to make the distinction between being a servant and being a slave. A true servant leader gets his marching orders from God. I'll say it again—it's important to remember that being a servant leader is about attitude first and then action.

It's not only possible, but also critical, that you maintain healthy boundaries while living out your servant leadership. Boundaries are like borders or guides. Think of driving on a mountain road—would you rather be driving on a road with guardrails or without? Boundaries tell you where to stop and start. They protect you. Setting boundaries in your life protects you, too. Being a servant leader is not about doing everything people want you to do. And it's not about doing everyone's work. It's more about giving of what you have—gifts, time, physical strength, wisdom—so you can help others give what they have. Having discernment means knowing when to say yes and when to say no, when to serve and when to allow others to serve.

Reread Ruth 3. How did Boaz exercise discernment?

Very early in the morning, while it was still dark, Jesus got up, left the house and went off to a solitary place, where he prayed. Simon and his companions went to look for him, and when they found him, they exclaimed: "Everyone is looking for you!"

Jesus replied, "Let us go somewhere else—to the nearby villages—so I can preach there also. That is why I have come." So he traveled throughout Galilee, preaching in their synagogues and driving out demons.

—MARK 1:35-39

Let's take a look at how Jesus does it. Read Mark 1:35-39. Jesus is very active in his ministry. He is healing, teaching, and casting out demons in the busy town of Capernaum. His fame is growing. His disciples are becoming excited about the ministry, seeing how the news of Jesus is spreading so quickly. There is plenty of work to be done there; plenty of people still need to be healed or taught. Everyone is anxious for more of him. And what does Jesus do? He spends the morning in prayer, getting the plan from the Master Planner himself. It seems obvious to the disciples that Jesus needs to get back in there—"Everyone is looking for you!" But Jesus says no to what is good so he can say yes to what is right. God tells him he needs to move on.

I learned this lesson the hard way. During my first few years in ministry, I wanted to be the ultimate servant leader. I thought whenever an opportunity to serve presented itself to me, I had to be there. Day after day the phone rang with people needing to talk, needing a ride, or needing some prayer. I almost never said no. If someone called at 10 o'clock at night because they were having a rough time, I ran right over to offer prayer and comfort. When the phone rang during my quiet time in the morning, I answered it. There wasn't an hour of my day that was off-limits to people. You can probably guess what happened—I started to burn out.

Soon, whenever the phone rang and someone needed me, my stomach tensed up. I found myself caring less—not more—for people. I couldn't even discern what to do about the way I was feeling because my habit of meeting with God every morning had been swallowed up by "serving him." I found myself in a place where every day I was busy talking to people about God, but I hadn't read my Bible for any meaningful length of time for weeks. I was dry, bitter, and ready to give up. Finally, I realized that in the condition I was in, I was of no use to anyone—especially God. So I finally asked for help. To make a long story short, I made some significant changes and began the process of learning to serve in a healthy way. How arrogant of me to think I could do what Jesus wouldn't do! I had to learn to get away to that quiet place on a regular basis and allow my Master Planner to tell me when to "move on to the next town," just as he did for Jesus.

So the bottom line is this—as leaders, we need to be ready to serve when God asks us. That means we need to have the right attitude—one that relinquishes pride and position, commits to go the extra mile, and prepares to count the cost of serving. It also means we listen with a discerning ear to what God asks us to do, instead of plowing ahead with our own agendas. We don't serve in order to manipulate, to gain the approval or love of others, or to further our own ambitions. We stay focused on the mission. We are here to serve only the Creator of the universe.

Who Is the Servant-Leader?

The servant-leader is servant first... It begins with the natural feeling that one wants to serve, to serve first. Then conscious choice brings one to aspire to lead. He or she is sharply different from the person who is leader first, perhaps because of the need to assuage an unusual power drive or to acquire material possessions. For such it will be a later choice to serve—after leadership is established.

The leader-first and the servant-first are two extreme types. Between them there are shadings and blends that are part of the infinite variety of human nature.

The difference manifests itself in the care taken by the servant—first to make sure that other people's highest priority needs are being served.

The best test, and difficult to administer, is: do those served grow as persons; do they, while being served, become healthier, wiser, freer, more autonomous, more likely themselves to become servants? And, what is the effect on the least privileged in society; will they benefit, or, at least, will they not be further deprived?

— ROBERT K. GREENLEAF, **SERVANT AS LEADER**

TAKE IT DEEPER

LEARN TO SERVE OTHERS

Do some experiments this week to practice taking these steps. Try to do as many of these things as you can.

- Ask your best friends to help you check your attitude. Give them permission to ask you to serve them in different ways throughout the week and then pay close attention to your attitude. Are you getting resentful? Irritated? Tired of it?

- Do what you can to work toward the cure for the "disease of me." Put a quarter in a jar every time you catch yourself trying to take care of yourself first. You know what I mean—stuff such as trying to grab the biggest cookie on the plate, getting a good spot in the lunch line, scoring that premium parking spot.

- Go the extra mile for someone this week—when your mom asks you to clear the table after dinner, do the dishes, too! When your best friend asks you to loan her five bucks, give her 10 (and don't expect to get repaid). Pay close attention to opportunities to go that extra mile.

- Make a list of some of the things you value most—it might be stuff you own, or it might be watching your favorite TV show or listening to the style of music you like when you're in the car. Make sure you have at least five things on your list. Now plan a way to sacrifice at least one of those things for the sake of someone else. (For extra credit: Choose to make a sacrifice for someone who bugs you!)

- Spend extra time this week with your journal. Pay close attention to any leading to serve. Is your motivation on target? If you catch yourself serving to manipulate instead of from a serving attitude, write it down in your journal and then tell at least one person.

JOURNALING SNAPSHOTS

DAY 1

Read Daniel 6:20. What word does the king use to describe the way Daniel serves God? What word would someone use to describe the way you serve God? Use your journal entry today as a place to talk to God honestly about the way you serve him.

DAY 2

Read Philippians 2:5. What is your attitude? Ask God to reveal to you today what attitudes drive your behavior. Record what he reveals to you.

DAY 3

Read Isaiah 41:9. Underline the last section of this verse in your Bible. Write about the ways you know God has chosen you. If this seems hard, keep praying and ask him to show you the ways he's chosen you.

DAY 4

Read John 12:26. How are you following him? Are you where God is? What does that mean for you? Use your journal time today as a way for God to show you how to follow him.

DAY 5

The word *servant* is found 478 times in the NIV Bible. Use your index or concordance and look up at least five of those verses. Write a letter to God telling him about what you have learned in this study.

■ CHAPTER FIVE

THE INNER LIFE OF A LEADER

Have you owned your first car yet? If not, then you probably will before too long. Either way, you've hopefully figured out by now that what's inside a car (under the hood) is way more important than what is outside. There are a lot of little parts inside that all have to work in sync with one another. You could say they need to be *integrated* in order to work. The thing about all those integrated parts is that they have to be maintained. Sometimes all it takes is for one little belt to stop working, and then the whole car sits in the driveway.

One night I put my youngest son to bed a little late. Normally, we have a pretty time-consuming bedtime ritual. We read a little, talk about the day, pray, and get the requisite last-minute drink of water. That night I was way too tired, and I had a lot of unfinished work from the day. So I skipped most of the ritual, offering only a quick kiss and a prayer. Ten minutes after I'd shut off his light, Nick popped into the kitchen where I was working.

Frustrated, I said, "Nick, what are you doing out of bed?"

"You need to tuck me in."

"I *did* tuck you in."

"You only prayed with me. Words don't tuck."

It was one of those moments when I knew God was speaking to me through the mouth of my little guy. What Nick was really saying to me was, "Don't just tell me about God; *show* him to me. Spend time with me. I need your attention and your touch." All of that condensed into a three-word phrase—"Words don't tuck." Because I was tired from a long day, I didn't have the physical or emotional energy I needed to be able to give him what he needed from me at the time. It was a good reminder for me: It isn't enough to know *how* to lead others well; we also need to *do* it well.

And without properly tending to our inner lives, we won't have the ability to do *anything* well. Those we lead depend on us to take good care of ourselves so we can give them the leadership attention they require.

"Don't go where I can't follow!"

—SAMWISE GAMGEE,
THE LORD OF THE RINGS: THE RETURN OF THE KING

Let's go back to my hero, King David. Throughout his reign he had a vision. He wanted to build a temple for the ark of the covenant of God. He made plans to build it and spent years preparing for this monumental project, but God decreed otherwise. David had to pass the project on to his son Solomon, who would succeed him as king. What would you say to your son in a moment such as that? It is an opportunity for David to pass on not only the project, but also all of the wisdom he's accumulated along the way. This is what David says:

> So now I charge you in the sight of all Israel and of the assembly of the Lord, and in the hearing of our God: Be careful to follow all the commands of the Lord your God, that you may possess this good land and pass it on as an inheritance to your descendants forever. And you, my son Solomon, acknowledge the God of your father, and serve him with wholehearted

> devotion and with a willing mind, for the Lord searches every heart and understands every motive behind the thoughts. If you seek him, he will be found by you; but if you forsake him, he will reject you forever. Consider now, for the Lord has chosen you to build a temple as a sanctuary. Be strong and do the work. (1 Chronicles 28:8-10)

In other words, after everything David had been through, he narrows the important things in leadership to these seven: Obey God, give him credit for being God (in other words, keep your pride out of it), serve him with everything you have, keep your thoughts tuned into his (and be ready for him to speak to you), always be on the lookout for him, keep yourself strong, and *do the work.*

After giving Solomon more detailed instructions for the temple, he repeats one thing: Stay strong and do the work. This time he adds a word of encouragement: "Do not be afraid or discouraged, for the Lord God, my God, is with you. He will not fail you or forsake you until all the work for the service of the temple of the Lord is finished" (1 Chronicles 28:20).

Tending to your inner life is a project not unlike the building of the temple. It requires obedience, reliance on God, a willing mind, a searching heart, and the determination to stay strong and do the work. Let's get to it!

THE VISION

In order to do an effective job of tending to your inner life, you need a plan. The first step in any plan is the vision. You need to know where you are going before you can get there. David is absolutely crystal clear on the plans for the temple, but don't miss this point—"I have [the plan] in writing from the hand of the Lord upon me, and he gave me understanding in all the details of the plan" (1 Chronicles 28:19). What we are talking about here is not personal goal setting—it is listening to God for the details and understanding the plans he has for transforming you into a godly, kingdom leader. Don't you want to be in the exact place of leadership God wants you in? Isn't it totally cool to imagine that God has a vision that YOU are a part of, and he wants to let you in on it?

Later in this chapter you will begin constructing the vision and the plan for tending to your own inner life. For now begin to pray specifically that God will unfold all the details of the plan to you.

"What I really lack is to be clear in my mind what I am to do, not what I am to know...The thing is to understand myself, to see what God really wishes me to do...to find the idea for which I can live and die."
—SOREN KIERKEGAARD, *JOURNAL*

SELF-LEADERSHIP

Dee Hock, founder and president emeritus of VISA Corporation and author of several books on the topic of corporate leadership, contends that all leaders must first lead themselves.

Now let's be real. When you think of who a leader leads, you think of followers, right? In your mind's eye you see yourself confidently heading toward that vision, and you turn around and see a bunch of people happily following you. You think *that* is what the work of leadership is, right? Well, Mr. Hock, a person with some pretty hefty experience in this area, has news for you: Although managing those we call "followers" is the focus of most of our thinking about leadership, Hock says the first and most important responsibility of anyone with influence over others is to manage one's self. The practice of *self-leadership*, or tending to one's own inner life, should occupy 50 percent—yes, half—of a leader's time and resources. If you haven't caught on yet, that is what this chapter is about: Getting to that place where you are doing the best job possible at leading your self so you can, in turn, do the best job possible leading others.

I won't lie to you. This is tough. It's always tempting for leaders to skip this stuff. The work you are about to do requires a lot of thought and focus. But trust me, if you make the work in this chapter a habit—something you regularly do over the course of your life—you and those around you will reap the benefits.

Okay, in order for you to truly invest in tending your inner life, first you have to answer some "Why?" questions. Unless you totally understand why you must give half of your time and attention to leading yourself, you won't get too far into the how of it. Take a break at this point in the chapter and work through these questions.

How authentic am I? Does my inner life match up with the person I present to others?

Who do I really want to be?

What qualities are important to me?

Why are those qualities important to me?

There is a great story about an old rabbi who lived in a monastery near the Russian border around the time of World War I. Having lived in seclusion nearly his entire life, the old rabbi was unaware of the chaos around him. One day he wandered away from the monastery a bit too far during his morning walk and inadvertently ended up at the Russian border crossing. The guard ran out and, with his gun pointed at the old rabbi's head, shouted, "Who are you and where are you going?"

The rabbi smiled weakly at the incensed guard. "How much do they pay you to guard this border?" he asked.

"Visions are born in the soul of a man or woman who is consumed with the tension between what is and what could be."
—ANDY STANLEY, **VISIONEERING**

The guard lowered his gun a little, then asked suspiciously, "Very little. Why do you want to know?"

"Because," the old rabbi answered gently, "I would be willing to pay you twice that to come to me each morning and ask me that same question."

So how would you answer that guard's question? Do you truly know who you are and where you're going? When you ask yourself why you should invest the time and energy it takes to lead yourself effectively, go back to these questions. Why should you? Because unless you do, you will never really know who you are or where you are going.

FROM THE *WHY* TO THE *HOW*

Before we get going on the *how* of tending your inner life, let's be really clear about something. Your inner self consists of more than just your spiritual self. When we talk about tending the inner life of a Christian leader, the mind immediately leaps to spiritual disciplines such as solitude, Bible reading, and prayer. While these are certainly essential ingredients, it's critical that we understand that a leader must tend to the whole self. We are physical, emotional, spiritual, and intellectual beings. God says we are to love him with our hearts, souls, minds, and strengths (Mark 12:30). Since he said it, we have to assume he really means it—so that seems a good place to start. Let's break these four areas down and see how you can lead yourself—excellently!—in each of these parts.

PHYSICAL SELF-LEADERSHIP

"You do not belong to yourself, for God bought you with a high price. So you must honor God with your body" (1 Corinthians 6:19-20, NLT).

We get a lot of our best leadership instructions from Paul. He has a lot to say about self-leadership of our physical bodies. Listen to this: "So I run straight to the goal with purpose in every step. I am not like a boxer who misses his punches. I discipline my body like an athlete, training it to do what it should. Otherwise, I fear that after preaching to others I myself might be disqualified" (1 Corinthians 9:26-27, NLT).

Why would Paul fear he would be disqualified if he hadn't disciplined his body?

You can exercise leadership over your physical self in many ways. Keeping your body healthy through good nutrition and exercise is an obvious one, but how are you doing with it? Obesity is a serious problem in our nation, as is lack of exercise. The slang term *couch potato* has actually made it into the dictionary. No kidding! Look at how many of our culture's leaders have been taken down by substance abuse. The stresses and demands of leadership can make leaders very vulnerable to the temptation of instant relaxation offered by drugs, tobacco, or alcohol.

Taking care of yourself physically also means getting enough rest and recreation. By our very nature leaders tend to be doers and can have a hard time learning when to shut it down for the day. Getting to bed at a reasonable hour on a regular basis and learning to read your body's signals for more rest are critical if you intend to make it for the long haul. Have you ever thought of playing as spiritual? Well, it is. Recreation literally means "to re-create." So when you play, you are re-creating yourself. How cool is that?

One more thing, leader: Sexual purity falls under this category as well. Uncontrolled lust has been the downfall of many great leaders. Don't fool yourself here. You are the only steward of your physical body, and allowing it to be degraded through improper sexual activity can destroy it. I probably don't need to tell you how tempting it is to keep this part of your inner life totally hidden. If this is an area of struggle for you (and it is for most of us!), take care of it. Find someone you can trust to hold you accountable. Confess stuff to that person regularly. Get real with God about it.

Which of the following tend to be areas of struggle for you: nutrition, exercise, substance abuse, rest, recreation, sexual purity?

What practical steps can you take to gain more control over each area?

EMOTIONAL SELF-LEADERSHIP

Learning how to control our emotions is one of the hardest areas of self-leadership. More leaders have experienced failure in leadership as a result of poor emotional management than lack of skill.

One of my first jobs was at a store at the local mall. My boss was an incredibly ambitious guy. He wanted our store first in sales—every sales period—and he wouldn't accept anything less. He demanded perfection and long hours from all the employees in the store. He was hard to work for because of his demands, but it was ultimately his loss of control over his emotional life that did him in. We had a very mediocre fall season that year, and when the numbers came in, it wasn't good. The day the report arrived, my boss spent the morning going over and over the reports in the back room. I was checking customers out at the front desk when he came storming up to the counter. It was the Christmas season, and the store was full. Three of us were working the registers, and there were lines in front of each one. The three of us, along with our shocked customers, watched in amazement as he blasted into the space behind the counter, grabbed the calculator (which at that time was about the size of a bathroom scale), furiously punched in some numbers, and let out a loud scream. He then threw the calculator on the floor and began to jump up and down on it, rendering it into a pile of springs and plastic pieces. A hush came over the store as we all watched to see what he was going to do next. He finally stopped and returned to the back of the store in a huff.

That tantrum was his professional undoing. Of course we lost a few customers that day, but it was worse than that. He lost all that remained of the respect his employees had for him. One called the corporate office and reported the incident. After that he was fired. I don't know what happened to him, but I hope he got some help. You see, an incident such as that doesn't just happen to a person. He had likely mismanaged his emotional life for a long time, and when a crisis hit, he was unable to handle it. His emotions got the best of him, and he went over the edge.

It's really worth it to do a ruthless examination of your emotional maturity. Do you struggle with fear? Are you crippled by frustration or anger? Do you find yourself feeling jealous of other people? Do you struggle with depression? Often leaders get in trouble when the emotional pendulum swings too far one way or the other. We all experience emotions, and even the negative ones are a normal part of life. Where you get into trouble is when emotions have a major impact on the way you live your life, either by overemphasizing them or denying them.

■■■ TAKE IT DEEPER

HOW MATURE ARE YOU?

Check out www.emotionallyhealthychurch.com. Download and print the "Inventory of Spiritual/Emotional Maturity" self-test under the "Helpful Materials" pull-down menu and take the test. When you're finished, highlight the three areas where you scored the lowest. Use these as guides when you're making your emotional self-leadership plan later on in this chapter.

INTELLECTUAL SELF-LEADERSHIP

"Mom, can I quit school?" This question prompted my mother's sharp response, "Why would you want to do something like that? You have a lot more learning to do!" I could see she didn't understand. But I couldn't think of anything else I needed to know. I had already learned everything: I could read and write; I knew all about my home state—in fact, I could name the other 49 states as well; I could even identify several birds just by their call. Here I was in the middle of the third grade, and I was faced with nine more wasted years spent learning stuff I already knew. I thought it was time to stop learning.

I guess it probably goes without saying that I'm glad my mom didn't let me quit school in the third grade. I have actually learned a few things since then. I'm committed to being a lifelong learner. In fact, the older I get, the more I realize how much I don't know and how badly I want to know it.

"Leadership cannot really be taught. It can only be learned."
—HAROLD S. GENEEN,
FORMER PRESIDENT AND CEO OF ITT,
WWW.THINKEXIST.COM

It has been said that the minute leaders stop learning, they stop leading. I believe that statement is absolutely true. By its very nature, the term "leader" implies motion. Change. Going somewhere. Investing time in your own personal growth is one of the most important jobs of a leader. In the book of Proverbs, Solomon says we should search for wisdom and understanding as earnestly as we would look for buried treasure (Proverbs 2:1-6).

Imagine if you found out that a century ago someone buried a box of silver in your backyard. Would you ignore it, considering the search too boring? Would you be bored if you pulled that box out of the ground and pried open the top for the first time? Learning should provoke the same feelings within you. Adding to your understanding about the world and the people in it is like an endless search for buried treasure.

As a leader you should constantly be striving to understand the people you lead. Listening to others and studying the biographies of those who have gone before us can help us understand people who think differently from the way we do—and can help us learn from their mistakes, too. Studying our culture by staying on top of current events helps us make wise decisions and create a vision for the future. Reading newspapers and magazines and talking with others helps enlarge our understanding of our world. Studying other cultures helps us understand the perspective of God and the urgency of the Great Commission. Exposure to fine arts challenges our creativity and gets us in touch with God the Creator. Do you like only one kind of music? Challenge yourself to spend time exposing yourself to other forms. Go to a symphony or to a jazz show. When is the last time you went to an art gallery? Or the theater? The arts can transport us to cultures and eras that are not our own. Even if you are not an artistic person, don't neglect this area of your intellectual growth.

What are you doing to challenge yourself intellectually?

Do you consider yourself a learner? Why?

How can you more effectively lead yourself intellectually?

SPIRITUAL SELF-LEADERSHIP

> *"Since we are surrounded by such a great cloud of witnesses, let us throw off everything that hinders and the sin that so easily entangles, and let us run with perseverance the race marked out for us" (Hebrews 12:1).*

Remember the story of the tortoise and the hare? They both finished the race, but they finished it very differently. The tortoise "ran" with perseverance and steadiness, staying with it until the end. The hare ran hard and furious for a while and then stopped for a little nap because he was so confident in his ultimate victory—like so many of us in our spiritual races. We run in furious spurts, full of energy and confidence. We have a wonderful mountaintop experience that feeds us, and then we take a breather, living off the energy of that time. We doze off spiritually, getting bored with our routine or overconfident in our spiritual condition. We take a break. Then, like the hare, we wake up in horror, realizing we have lost ground and need to run like crazy to catch up.

Have you run your spiritual race like that? You may not "lose" the race, as the hare did, because your race is run not against others but for the sake of finishing well. But when you run your spiritual race like the hare, you risk finishing poorly or not finishing like you should. As a spiritual leader, imagine those in your charge following you as you run the race. Not only do you want to finish well, but you want those you are leading to finish well, too.

Think about your spiritual race. How would you describe the course so far?

If there were a news report covering your race, how would it read?

For the last few years my husband has participated in a unique form of torture (at least that's how I view it!)—a triathlon. The contestants swim for a half-mile (across a lake and back), bike for 18 miles, and then run for five miles. He was quite happy with his finishing time this year, having knocked off three minutes from his last race. And he's learned a few things about running this kind of race—stuff that's probably not too different from what might help you run your spiritual race.

Being prepared

There is no doubt that one of the most important aspects of running a good race is training—consistent, challenging training. You don't just wake up one morning and decide to do a triathlon. Rob spent months running, swimming, and biking. He had to make sacrifices to fit it into his schedule. He had to commit to it daily, whether he felt like it or not. He needed the right equipment—the wrong shoes or tires on his bike could make a huge difference in his time and even in his ability to finish.

What does it mean to be well-prepared for your race?

What does your training routine look like?

What kind of equipment do you need to run your race?

Getting rid of hindrances

My husband learned there were some things that could get in the way of his training. He had to find ways to train even when the weather prevented him from going outside. If he didn't, it would have become too easy for him to train only when it was convenient, and then he'd get out of the habit of his daily discipline. He had to make his training a priority because his schedule could become a hindrance if he allowed it to.

What things hinder you?

Is there sin in your life that tangles you up and prevents you from running well?

Support from others

It helped Rob to tell others about his goal of doing the triathlon and talk to others who had done it before. He needed their words of wisdom and inside knowledge of things to watch out for. During the event itself the shouts of encouragement from the spectators along the sidelines were the only things keeping him going during some of the race's tougher moments. If he had been running alone on a quiet street, he might never have made it to the finish line.

The companionship with the other runners gave him motivation to give it all he had. This year there was a guy who was running at the same pace as Rob through most of the event. One would pull in front of the other for a few moments, which prompted the other to push a little harder and nudge into the lead. Back and forth they went throughout the two-hour competition. They finished very close to one another, and when they crossed the finish line, they shook hands and smiled at one another. Then they began to compare stories of their shared experience—"I thought you were going to lose me on the third hill;" "I could hear you behind me as I made the turn."

We don't run our spiritual races alone, either. We encourage each other, pull each other up, and spur each other on to run harder. When we run our races in *community* with others, we increase our chances of finishing well.

Are you regularly spending time with others, encouraging each other spiritually?

With whom are you sharing your race experience? How are you keeping each other in the race?

Commitment

There were many times when Rob was tempted to forget the whole idea of participating in the triathlon—when the weather was rotten, when his knees hurt, when there was something else he wanted to do, or when he just plain got sick of it. And in the end there was only one thing that kept him going: He was committed to doing it. He had fixed his eyes on the finish line long before the actual race started. He set a goal and committed to it. He filled out a race form, paid an entry fee, told others about his goal, and then he ran toward it. He persevered in his pursuit of his goal.

Commitment plays a big role in our spiritual race as well. In the Hebrews passage we are encouraged to "run with perseverance." What comes next? "Let us fix our eyes on Jesus, the author and perfecter of our faith" (Hebrews 12:2).

We do get tired, bored, and tempted to stop training. How can we persevere when all we can think of is quitting? What keeps us focused on our commitment? Keeping our eyes on Jesus. Remembering who he is and what he did for us. When I get tired, I think about who I am as a child of God. When I remember that, I'm also reminded that I can't give up. He won't let me. He will pursue me until I get back in the race. I belong to him. I want to spend eternity ruling and reigning with Christ—I am in this for the long haul.

What keeps you committed to your spiritual race?

What are things you think about or do to keep your focus on Jesus?

Being willing to pay the price
Running a triathlon is not cheap. Picking up a pair of shoes off the clearance table at a discount store doesn't cut it. Good shoes that fit well, a good bike with appropriate tires, water bottles, running clothes, a racing suit for the swim, entry fees—the list goes on. That is just the monetary cost. The time for training and the pain of sore muscles and injuries cost a lot as well. Before making the commitment to run the race, you need to be willing to pay the price.

You will pay a price for running your spiritual race well, too. It is different for everyone, but you will most assuredly need to count the cost. Counting the cost for you may mean time and resources invested in preparation and study, financial sacrifice, even persecution and rejection.

What is the price you pay to stay on course spiritually?

What happens when you avoid paying the full cost of your spiritual race?

When the psalmist tells us David led with "integrity of heart," he is telling us David led with all of himself—even the hidden parts. There was integration, or integrity, of the physical, emotional, intellectual, and spiritual parts of David. He managed those parts of himself well and led out of what resulted—an integrated heart.

HOW IS YOUR BALANCE?

Have you ever played that game at an amusement park where all the little frogs pop out of the "pond" one at a time, and you have to whack them back down with a mallet? After a while you find yourself wildly swinging at every hint of movement. Self-leadership can feel that way when we get out of balance or out of control. When we neglect an area for too long, the effort it takes to get back into balance can cause us to neglect others and can create a feeling of being "out of whack."

Review your answers to the "self-leadership" questions and then evaluate on a scale of 1-10 how much effort, time, and resources you believe you've devoted to each area in the past month or so. A ranking of 1 means "I haven't devoted anything to this yet"; a 10 means "I've given it my all."

Then for each of the four self-leadership areas represented on the graph below, use a pencil or pen to shade in the corresponding bars above "Effort," "Time," and "Resources" to represent your level of involvement to this point.

10												
9												
8												
7												
6												
5												
4												
3												
2												
1												
	Effort	Time	Resources	Effort	Time	Resources	Effort	Time	Resources	Effort	Time	Resources
	PHYSICAL SELF-LEADERSHIP			**EMOTIONAL SELF-LEADERSHIP**			**INTELLECTUAL SELF-LEADERSHIP**			**SPIRITUAL SELF-LEADERSHIP**		

When you've finished filling in the graph, examine the results again.

In the four areas of self-leadership, how balanced is your life?

FINDING THE BALANCE

You may have noticed that this is the longest chapter in the book. That was very intentional on my part. This chapter, which is about your heart, is the very heart of this book. When it comes to leading with integrity of heart, you've got to start from a healthy place. If you integrate all the parts of an untended inner life, you won't end up with a heart capable of sustaining good leadership.

Learning to tend your inner life is so critical that it's worth investing the time it takes for ruthless examination and planning. Okay, grab yourself a snack and get going!

JOURNALING SNAPSHOTS

DAY 1

Read Matthew 6. What do you do outwardly that you should only be doing inwardly?

DAY 2

Read Mark 10:17-27. Jesus shows love to the rich young man by giving him an assignment. In your journal today respond as if Jesus gave that assignment to you.

DAY 3

Read Jeremiah 3:15. You can only lead with wisdom and understanding if you are also learning something. Write about what God has been teaching you.

DAY 4

Read Psalm 103. Choose at least one verse from this passage that jumps out at you. Use your journal to record what God says to you through this verse.

DAY 5

Read Nehemiah 6:1-9. Satan often tries to sidetrack us from the work we are doing. Record the ways you see him trying to get you off track and how you are resisting him.

PART TWO

...with skillful hands he led them

■ CHAPTER SIX

THE LISTENING LEADER

There's nothing like the embarrassment when, during a conversation, the other person says, "What do *you* think?" and you realize you haven't heard a word he said. Ouch! Listening is something we all take for granted. Very seldom do we really work at it, giving it our full time and attention. When was the last time you thought about your listening *skills?* Did you know that when people are surveyed about what they consider the most important leadership qualities, "good listener" is always at the very top of the list? People want—actually need—to be listened to. When people know someone is really listening to what they are saying, they feel respected, honored, and accepted.

My little brother was a chronic talker. He never shut up from the moment of his birth. We begged my mom to make him be quiet. One of our favorite childhood stories is about the time we were driving home from a family vacation in my parents' brand-new car. My brother was in the back seat with my sister and me, and he was blabbing on and on as usual. Out of necessity we'd developed the ability to be in the same space with him and not hear a single thing he was saying. But this time he must have been looking for some feedback from us because suddenly he yelled, "Hey, no one is listening to me! You guys need to listen to me!" We all just kept on doing whatever we were doing. I kept reading, my sister kept dozing, and my parents continued their conversation in the front seat.

"Hey, you guys need to listen to me!" he insisted. "If you don't listen to me, I'm gonna throw up!" No one even looked at him. He repeated the threat—louder this time. And of course we all continued to ignore him.

When he saw no one was listening to him *still*, he let it rip—all over the back seat and floor of my dad's new car. Now he had our attention. I laughed my head off, my sister screamed, and my parents fumed. Steve smiled and said, "Are you going to listen to me now? I want to know when we're going to stop for lunch!"

Thankfully, we all laugh now when we tell that story. Can't you feel how desperately he wanted someone to listen to him? That desperation is true of everyone. We all long to have someone listen to us.

Proverbs 1:5 says, "Let the wise listen and add to their learning." In the last chapter we explored the importance of being a lifelong learner. Wise leaders add to their learning by listening. No one has "enough" wisdom and understanding that they can't learn *something* by listening to someone else. We always have something else to learn—actually, in most cases we still have a *whole lot to learn.*

In a sense being a poor listener is a form of pride. If a leader doesn't deliberately work to develop her listening skills, she is displaying an arrogant belief in herself. Learning to listen well can be a secret weapon. The best leaders are constantly listening and learning. Have you ever stopped to think that every person you will ever meet knows something you don't know? One of the ways a leader can lead with an integrated heart is to make it a priority to constantly grow and learn by listening.

ARE YOU A GOOD LISTENER?

It is said that 85 percent of people would rate their listening abilities as average to poor. If you've ever played the telephone game, you probably agree with this statistic. Remember sitting in a circle while one person whispers something in the ear of the person next to him, and on it goes around the circle? By the time it makes it all the way back to the beginning, what might have started as "Once upon a time there were three bears" somehow ends up as "One pound of time for free éclairs."

How good a listener are you? Do you often find yourself in misunderstandings with others? Do you have trouble remembering what people say to you? How well do you stay focused on others while they are talking? Even if you would consider yourself a really good listener, let me challenge you as a learning leader to become even better!

THE STEPS OF LISTENING

Listening well is more than just receiving sounds in our ears. Good listening takes intentional work and lots of practice. Look through these steps and ask yourself how many of these things you do well.

1. Quieting—William Isaacs said, "To listen is to develop an inner silence." Have you ever paid attention to how truly noisy and chaotic your mind can get? When another person begins to speak to you, you need to quiet the inner chaos of your mind and prepare to listen.

2. Presence—Listening well requires that you are truly present with the person you are listening to. That means you are with him where he is. It means you aren't mentally off in some other time or place. There is a great book by Mike Mason called *Practicing the Presence of People*, which really helps the reader understand not only the importance of being present with people, but how to practice it as well. Check it out!

3. Content—If you want to avoid making a really intelligent response such as "Huh?" then you need to listen for content. The physical act of truly hearing another person requires that you pay attention to what she is saying and absorb all the information she is sharing with you.

4. Understanding—It's critical that you understand what the speaker is trying to say to you. Be aware that you are interpreting everything you hear through your own experience, knowledge, and attitudes. If you don't understand something that's been said, it's important that you ask the speaker to clarify it for you. Most people won't think you're being rude if you ask for clarification. In fact, it can actually make the other person feel ***more*** listened to.

5. Interpretation—As you listen, you need to evaluate what you're hearing. You may need to decide whether or not you believe the information is true or whether you need *more* information.

6. Response—The final step is to respond to what you've heard. This lets the speaker know you've heard him, and it also gives him the opportunity to make sure you haven't misunderstood what he said. Providing feedback shows the speaker respect. Have you ever spoken to a person who gave no response whatsoever? Didn't you just want to scream, "Hello?! Are you there?" A good way to respond is to reflect back what you heard: "So what I'm hearing you say is…" Even if you don't *like* what a person has said, make sure you respond in a way that lets him know you've listened to him.

BARRIERS TO LISTENING

Listening well is hard work. It's active, not passive. Unfortunately, many personal habits and patterns can prevent us from listening and communicating well. Learning to avoid some of the common barriers to good listening can help you be a more effective communicator.

These are some patterns to watch out for:

1. Comparing yourself to the speaker. (My experience was harder than that.)
2. Reading the speaker's mind instead of listening to what he's really saying. (I'll bet he thinks I'm going to be mad at him.)
3. Planning what you're going to say next. (As soon as he stops talking, I'm going to share this great story.)
4. Filtering out the things you don't want to hear or think about.
5. Judging what the person is saying before she finishes saying it. (I'm not listening to any more of this. It's stupid.)
6. Losing focus by daydreaming and getting lost in your own thoughts.
7. Challenging every statement as if you're in a debate with the speaker.
8. Shutting down your mind, believing you already know what the speaker is going to say.
9. Changing the topic instead of responding.
10. Placating the other person by nodding or saying, "Uh-huh," without really processing whether or not you agree.
11. Using poor eye contact and body language, which communicates disinterest. If you are looking around at everything but the person who is talking, you are disconnected from him.

—Adapted from *Messages: The Communications Skill Book* by Matthew McKay, Martha Davis, and Patrick Fanning

Okay, stop here. Don't move on to the next section just yet. Take a moment and look back through the list of patterns. Be brutally honest with yourself and circle the numbers of all the bad habits and patterns you can identify with—things you've done when you should have been actively listening instead. Pick your top three (or worst three) and then keep those negative patterns in mind this week as you practice better listening habits.

HOW LEADERS LISTEN

Do leaders have to listen differently than other people? Absolutely! Think about all the things leaders are called to do. Among others we've talked about serving and praying. In the next few chapters we'll talk about vision casting, teaching, coaching, managing conflict, and mentoring. Of course leaders do a ton of other stuff, too, but just think about each one of those things I listed and imagine how effective a person's leadership would be in those areas if they were a lousy listener.

Good listening is about way more than just hearing the words a person is saying. Earlier in the chapter I talked about how important it is that leaders are good listeners so they can be good learners. I really can't stress this enough—you don't know everything you need to know. If you are going to lead well, you have to listen well so you know *how* to lead.

Okay, so if you're not just listening for people's words, what are you listening for? Here are a few things:

- Content—The obvious one. What information is this person imparting to you? Could you accurately retell it to another person? If so, you've done a good job of listening for content.

- Emotions—This is a bit trickier, as people usually communicate some kind of emotion when they're talking. Are they fearful? Nervous? Happy? Excited?

Keying into a person's emotions is a helpful skill for leaders to have. For instance, let's say you're leading an event-planning team. One of the team members is reporting her progress to you. If you just listened for content, you could safely say things were going fine. But if you listened for underlying emotions, you might pick up on the fact that she's angry. You can then ask her a couple of questions to help you get the information you really need to lead well.

- Intention—Whenever someone communicates with you, he has an intention. Sometimes the intention is to make you laugh or cry; sometimes it's to give you information; sometimes he wishes to receive advice or feedback from you. When leaders listen for intention, they know how to respond appropriately. Did you ever tell someone a story while fully expecting a "Hey, awesome!" kind of response but then received some advice from the listener instead? How likely are you to follow that advice? Probably not very. It may even have been good advice, but when the response doesn't match your intention, it shuts you down. It's good for leaders to work hard at listening for a speaker's intention. And if you can't tell what his intention is—ask! Especially if you think he is asking for feedback of some kind. Say something such as, "Are you looking for some advice?" If he says no, tuck it away and find another time to bring it up.

- Revelation—Besides emotion and intent, people often reveal a lot of themselves in their communication. Leaders should listen carefully for those revelations in order to get to know the people they're leading. Remember all that work you did at the beginning of the book to discover your temperament, gifts, and learning styles? You should also know that stuff about the people you lead. Sprinkled all throughout your conversations with people are little clues about who they really are. Good leaders are the ones who are good at detecting those clues and putting them all together.

LISTENING TO GOD

Listening to others is a critical skill for leaders, but we shouldn't neglect putting forth the effort to listen to God as well. God speaks to us in many ways. Scripture is packed with admonitions to *listen to the Lord*—and also to listen to others because he speaks to us through his people.

Remember the story of young Samuel? He is just lying in his bed when he hears his name being called over and over again. He thinks it's his guardian, Eli. So he keeps running to Eli's room, only to be told Eli never said anything. After Samuel wakes Eli up a few times, it finally occurs to Eli that Samuel is hearing God speak to him. Eli advises Samuel to go back to bed once more. If God should call to him again, then Samuel should answer this way, "Speak, Lord, your servant is listening." So Samuel does just that, and God has a lot to say to him. Is that your response, too? How often do you quiet yourself and invite God to speak to you by saying, "Speak, Lord, for your servant is listening" (1 Samuel 3:9)?

For weeks a friend of mine was hearing the same song playing over and over again in her head. She was starting to get really annoyed because she didn't recognize the tune, and it wouldn't go away. Then one morning she finally recognized it as a Christmas song she learned as a child. *Why in the world am I hearing this song in my head?* she wondered. Then it occurred to her that God might be trying to speak to her. She did some digging and found the lyrics to the song. She'd never really paid attention to the words before, but the song was the story of a good king who reaches out to the poor in his kingdom. So she felt God put that song in her head to spur her on to be a blessing to the poor in her community. As she read the words to the song, it was as if it had been written just for her and with answers to her questions. God had been singing that song over her! Because she had learned to pay attention to those little things and listen, she didn't miss this beautiful gesture of love from God.

One of my biggest parental frustrations occurs when I find out my kids haven't done something I've asked them to do. Later when I ask them again why those things still haven't been done, I get this response: "Oh, I didn't hear you." I go nuts! How often have my kids missed out on learning some good things because they didn't listen closely? Do you ever do that to your mom? Have you learned how to tune out the things or the people you don't want to hear? When I first meet God when I get to heaven, I don't want to hear him ask me, "Why didn't you do...?" and then have to respond lamely, "I didn't hear you." I want to learn how to be a good listener now.

I Blew It by Not Listening Well!

About two years ago I had a friend who wasn't the coolest, most popular kid in the class. But he wanted to learn more about Jesus, and he knew I knew about Jesus. He kept asking and asking to sit with me at lunch and asking me what church I went to. I didn't know he was asking about Christ. The only thing I saw in him was a video game-loving geek.

Eventually he moved away. I kept thinking about him. I felt so weird because my conscience was killing me. Three months ago I realized he was calling for Christ. I felt so badly. I wish so much that I could have told him about Christ! If I could go back in time, I would go back to fifth grade and share with him everything about Jesus that I know.

—CRAIG S., 13

LISTENING WELL TO GOD

A friend once put it this way: "You know when you pick up the phone and the person says, 'Hi!' and you just know who he is by the sound of his voice? That's because you talk to him so often, you're able to recognize his voice right away. I ask the Lord to speak to me often until I can recognize his voice as easily as my very best friend's." I love that! Here are some helpful things to keep in mind as you learn to listen well to God. You will notice they are very similar to the skills that enable you to listen well to others.

1. Quiet—Make time and space for quieting your mind and body.

2. Pay attention—God may be speaking to you through some unusual sources. Be on the lookout for ways he is trying to communicate with you.

3. Keep an open mind—Don't jump to conclusions about what you are expecting to hear or what you want to hear. Allow God to surprise you.

4. Write it down—If the creator of the whole universe had something to say just to you—wouldn't you want to remember it? It is so easy to forget the little

"Mind you, there are thousands of clever men who would give anything for the chance to come in and take over from me, but I don't want that sort of person. I don't want a grown-up person at all. A grown-up won't listen to me; he won't learn. He will try to do things his own way. So I have to have a child."

—Willy Wonka in **Charlie and the Chocolate Factory,** Roald Dahl

things. Keeping a journal or taking notes is key to good listening.

5. Evaluate well—Not every little thought that passes through your mind is from God. Praying about the things you hear, bouncing them off other mature believers, and staying in the Word of God (to learn and understand the character of God) are all-important and will help you discern what you are hearing.

6. Don't respond too soon—As in a conversation with a friend, if you are busy thinking about what you want to say next instead of listening to what your friend is saying, you'll miss what's truly being said. During your prayer time be sure you are spending enough time just quietly and expectantly listening to God.

7. Practice, practice, practice—The more you work on learning to listen, the better you'll become.

TAKE IT DEEPER

LISTENING SURVEY

Interview three students (ones who aren't also doing this exercise) about their listening behaviors. Encourage your respondents to be as specific as possible when answering. Be sure to write down their responses to each question. When you have completed all three of the interviews, write a summary of the interviews in your journal, noting the similarities and differences among the responses. In your summary include your discoveries about how people listen.

Interview Questions

1. Do you listen better in some classes than in others?
2. What physical characteristics in a classroom affect your listening ability the most?
3. What are the greatest barriers to your listening to a classroom lecture?
4. What helps you to listen well in the classroom?
5. How much of what you hear in a class do you remember?

Take It Even Deeper

For one whole day keep your journal with you. Begin your day with the prayer, "Speak, Lord, I am listening," and continue to pray it throughout the day. Pay close attention to your thoughts and the things you hear from others. And don't miss any messages in the music you listen to or in the things you read. In your journal, record everything you think may be from God—no matter how remote the possibility. At the end of the day, read through everything you've written, pray over it, and try to discern the things God has said to you throughout the day.

JOURNALING SNAPSHOTS

DAY 1

Read 1 Corinthians 13:1-3. Pray over this passage and ask God to show you the truth about how much love you have for others. In your journal honestly record what you hear.

DAY 2

Read 1 Corinthians 13:4-13. Read this passage aloud and replace the word *love* with your own name. How true is what you just read? Record in your journal the thoughts God brings to your mind as you read this passage with your name in it.

DAY 3

Read Revelation 11:3-6. God is ready to give you the power you need to do everything he asks you to do. Have you accepted that? Are you resisting his power in any way?

DAY 4

Read Proverbs 12:15. Do you listen to the advice of others? What have others been trying to tell you that you may not be listening to? How good are you at taking advice? Write about your own need to be right about things and ask for God's help in this area.

DAY 5

Read 1 Kings 10:1-13. People need to count on the wisdom of their leaders (v. 8). Are you continually seeking wisdom for your leadership? Write to God about it.

CHAPTER SEVEN

THE COMMUNICATING LEADER

"The Lord said to him, 'Who gave man his mouth? Who makes him deaf or mute? Who gives him sight or makes him blind? Is it not I, the Lord? Now go; I will help you speak and will teach you what to say.'"
—Exodus 4:11-12

Have you ever experienced miscommunication? Misheard someone or been misheard yourself? The ability to impart and receive information accurately is critical for any leader. You can possess a great vision, massive amounts of wisdom and knowledge, and sterling character, but if you can't impart those things to those you lead, you may as well be on a deserted island. In this lesson we're going to dive into one of the most important skills of a leader—the ability to communicate well. In the last lesson we explored the skill of listening. Now we're going to take a look at the other side of the coin—the ways we speak and communicate to others.

THE POWER OF THE SPOKEN WORD

"There is nothing new under the sun," the author of Ecclesiastes (1:9) writes, and he is absolutely correct. And what is the oldest thing under the sun? The spoken word. God spoke creation into being. God *said*, "Let there be..." over and over as the universe unfolded beneath his hands. Who can grasp the enormity of a universe created through the power of *words?* Yet the truth is that our almighty God is a communicator. He began the world with words, and he is still speaking to us today.

Find a partner—your friend, your mom—whoever is nearby. Look at one another for 30 seconds and try not to communicate anything. Can you do it? I bet you can't!

Because we are created in God's image, we are also communicators. Communication is a big part of God's strategy for saving mankind. He only sent Jesus to earth one time. He doesn't send him over and over again for each generation. Two thousand years after Christ's lifetime, millions of people still follow Jesus because someone has told them the story. Words matter.

Whether you consider yourself quiet and shy, a total chatterbox, or somewhere in between, you are a communicator. We all are. And we're always communicating something, whether or not we're trying to. Throughout this book we've been talking about your integrity of heart. That integrated heart is revealed to others through communication. In fact, communication might be the most important skill for a leader to develop, and like every other skill it takes lots of intentional practice to do it well.

GOD—THE GREAT COMMUNICATOR

When we look closely at the story of God in Scripture, we can see that from beginning to end God is modeling lots of things about communication. We can learn a lot just by noticing how God does it. Let's take a peek.

IT'S ABOUT THE RELATIONSHIP!

God totally loves people. The gospel itself is the longest-running love story there is. God is a relational, connecting God. Creating Adam was the greatest pleasure of all of his creation, the only thing he declared "very good." From that moment on God began an ongoing dialogue with his people. He started by walking in the garden with Adam and Eve. He met face to face with Moses, wrestled with Jacob, and sent Jesus in the flesh to touch and hold us in order to convey his love for us.

Not long ago I was visiting a church in California. I told a story about someone I know who experienced Jesus during the final moments before his close friend passed away. After I told the story, a guy in his early twenties came up to me with a smile on his face. He told me he was a Buddhist and that he had gone that day to see the movie *The Passion of the Christ*, which is a depiction of the last 12 hours of the life of Jesus. This is what he said to me: "I've never really been able to figure the whole Jesus thing out, but I think I get it now. Between the movie and this story I finally figured it out. God wanted to have a whole relationship with people. He wanted to touch them, look them in the eye when he talked to them, and really connect with them in a physical way. That's what Jesus is. Jesus is his touch connection to us!"

What that guy knew is that when you really love others, you want a connection with them. You want to communicate fully with them. Communication is a huge part of loving people. When God communicates with people, he reveals his personal relationship with them. His affirmations, blessings, and rebukes are all personal, revealing that he *knows and cares about* the people he is speaking to.

For leaders to communicate in relationship means they never forget the person they are talking to. Talking to others becomes less about transmitting information and more about sharing it with other human beings. It means considering how another person may be changed or affected by what you are communicating to him. It means taking the risk to be honest and open in your communication, revealing your true self. Communicating in relationship means speaking to others in a way that demonstrates that they are known.

Even with people you don't know personally, it's possible to communicate in a relational way. Have you ever experienced the checkout person at the mall who rings up your purchases, takes your money, and tells you to have a nice day while never bothering to look at you? *Being fully present with people—looking them in the eye, listening to their answers to your questions, responding appropriately—reflects the character of God.* Every person a leader communicates with is worthy of that leader being sacrificially and fully present with him.

When you communicate with others, are you often more interested in hearing yourself talk than connecting in relationship to those you're talking with?

How present are you in your face-to-face conversations? Do you often "check out" when you are talking to others?

GOD COMMUNICATES WITH EXCELLENCE IN A VARIETY OF WAYS

He gives visions and dreams in which he reveals himself for warning or instruction. He speaks powerfully through nature, his very creation. He talks to us through people and corporately through the church. He speaks intimately to our hearts through thoughts and impressions. God also speaks to us through Scripture.

Leaders, too, need to communicate in a variety of ways. We can communicate with words, with music, even with silence. We communicate to others by the way we dress, by our facial expressions, by the tone of our voice. The wise leader pays attention to her body language and the message she is sending to others apart from her words. We've all experienced talking with people whose body language and tone of voice or facial expressions didn't match their words. Which message did you receive?

We live in an age in which the methods of communication have never been so vast. We can e-mail, instant message, page, talk on our cell phones, even write an old-fashioned card or letter. People are more accessible than ever to one another. That means leaders also need more discernment than ever before to know how to communicate effectively with those they lead. It also takes more effort to sharpen our different communication skills. It takes practice.

Many Web sites have posted various forms of the following humorous (but supposedly true) story about a wannabe bank robber in San Francisco. Consider the consequences of this guy's failure to sharpen his written communication skills:

A thief walked into the downtown Bank of America branch and wrote, "This iz a stikkup. Put all your muny in this bag." While standing in line, waiting to give his note to the teller, he began to worry that someone had seen him write the note and might call the police before he reached the teller window. So he left

Bank of America and crossed the street to Wells Fargo. After waiting a few minutes in line, he handed his note to the Wells Fargo teller. She read it, and surmising from his spelling errors that he wasn't the brightest light in the harbor, told him she could not accept his stickup note because it was written on a Bank of America deposit slip, and he would either have to fill out a Wells Fargo deposit slip or go back to Bank of America. Looking somewhat defeated, the man said, "Okay" and left. He was arrested a few minutes later waiting in line back at Bank of America.

Granted, the bank robber had a few other problems, too. Regardless, the teller was able to figure out quite a bit from a tiny piece of written communication. When we are sloppy or lax in our communication, we send a message.

Do you consistently work to improve your communication skills? How?

What is your weakest method of communication?

GOD IS A GREAT STORYTELLER

"The Divine Romance," as it's been called, is the greatest story ever told. What a beautiful gesture for God to record our history in the form of a story. From the days of creation to the final days in Revelation, a story has been unfolding that tops them all. There is romance and war, good and evil, destruction and redemption. God's story has it all.

During Jesus' time on earth he had a lot to communicate to mankind. He could have come and taught classes to outline all the rules and regulations required for us to be right with God. He could have given lists and policies and procedures to follow. He didn't. He told stories. He told them over and over and over again. He told stories so people could understand the deep and important things he had to say. He told stories because they transcend time—we can still relate to them today. Stories get passed down from person to person; lists of rules generally don't.

In his book *Aquachurch*, futurist Leonard Sweet says, "The art of telling stories is one of the paramount leadership tools of postmodern culture." To be a successful and effective leader in the present and coming era, you must master the art of storytelling.

Kingdom-building leaders move God's people to new places because the stories they tell are compelling enough to change for, gripping enough to die for. I once heard a speaker say, "Jesus was perfectly capable of laying out 'Five Principles to Dynamic Praying,' and the fact that he didn't should make us reflect." Jesus didn't tell stories to entertain people. He used them for the same purposes that you as a leader should tell them: to instruct, to challenge, and to illustrate difficult concepts.

Are you telling God's stories to those you lead in a compelling way?

Are the stories you tell more about God or more about you?

THE TRUTH, THE WHOLE TRUTH, AND NOTHING BUT THE TRUTH

God's character being what it is, he can only speak truth—he is truth. We can depend on what he tells us because we are confident that God speaks only truth. When God communicates, he does it in an authentic way. He doesn't reveal all things at all times, but what he does reveal is true.

I guess I don't need to tell you that lying isn't one of the behaviors found among great leaders. Your parents and teachers have probably warned you that telling lies will get you into big-time trouble. If we all know it's such a bad thing to do, then why do so many people struggle to tell the truth? For leaders it comes down to creating a good impression, protecting a reputation, getting ahead, staying in control—lots of things that leaders are tempted to put ahead of the sometimes-difficult job of telling the truth.

One of the big challenges to this whole concept of "truth" is—what is it? It's a big question that a lot of people are asking. How can anyone really know the truth? Well, no human can know the whole truth with a capital "T"—the kind where you know everything about the whole world all the time—only God gets to know that kind of Truth. And there are lots of other things we can only know partially.

It's really important that leaders understand this about truth—we all have to tell our stories in ways that are completely true, but none of us have the entire story to tell. That's why God communicates to communities as well as to people (which we'll talk more about in just a bit). So one of the arts of communicating is being able to fully communicate your stories in an authentic, true way, while still honoring others' stories.

So it's incredibly important for you as a leader to understand that you don't know it all. Part of integrating humility into your heart is to keep this in mind and ask God, "Show me what I can't see." At the same time, telling the real truth about what you do know is a challenge that sometimes calls for real courage. It helps a lot to take some time to evaluate how you do in this area. Before you go any further, work through the Take It Deeper questions.

TAKE IT DEEPER

GET REAL WITH YOURSELF

Take a few moments and ask God for the courage to answer these questions in an authentic way.

How am I tempted to behave badly when telling my stories—do I exaggerate, stretch the truth, withhold stuff, put my own spin on things?

How well can I tell the whole truth, as I know it, while honoring the stories of others? Do I secretly believe my story is the truest or the only truth?

How well do I tell myself the truth? Am I in denial about how I behave toward others or how my behavior affects others? Is my self-talk true or untrue? In other words, do I say things to myself such as, "I'm such a loser," which isn't true?

HE DOESN'T SKIP THE HARD STUFF

Confrontation is one of the most challenging jobs of leadership. If you're going to lead, you won't be able to get away without doing some confronting sometime. Most of us hate confrontation—we hate doing it, and we hate being confronted even more! I really think we hate it because most of the time it's done so badly. Good leaders take the time to learn how to confront well and receive confrontation even better. If it's done well, confrontation can actually bring people closer and make people feel loved and safe. You may now be thinking, *Huh? What planet are you on?*

Think about it for a moment. One of the most important things a leader does is establish trust. You won't do much leading without it, but building trust with someone is hard work. Think about the last confrontation you were a part of. How did it go? Have you given any thought to how it could have gone any better?

We are all instructed to speak the truth in love, but the leader is held to an even higher standard. When we see those whom we lead believing or speaking things that are untrue, we have a responsibility to point out the error and speak the truth. A word of warning here—speaking the truth requires *knowing* the truth. "Surely you desire truth in the inner parts; you teach me wisdom in the inmost place" (Psalm 51:6).

When we speak God's truth to others, not our own personal opinions or preferences, we honor God and others. The only way to know God's truth is to allow God entrance into our innermost places—our hearts. We must study God's Word and voraciously pursue truth in all things. This is easier said than done, even in Jeremiah's day. Look what God tells Jeremiah: "If you can find but one person who deals honestly and seeks the truth, I will forgive this city" (Jeremiah 5:1).

Do you think our honesty and truthfulness are important to God? He was willing to forgive an entire city if he could find just one person who sought the truth. When Paul is giving Timothy his list of qualifications for leaders in the church, he includes, "They must keep hold of the deep truths of the faith with a clear conscience" (1 Timothy 3:9).

How passionately do you pursue truth?

"The heavens declare the glory of God; the skies proclaim the work of his hands. Day after day they pour forth speech; night after night they display knowledge. There is no speech or language where their voice is not heard. Their voice goes out into all the earth, their words to the ends of the world."

—PSALM 19:1-4

Do you test things to make sure they are true before you pass them on to others?

How is your ability to speak the truth in love—even in difficult circumstances?

Communication is a huge subject. You're not going to get everything you need to know or consider about communication in this little chapter—that's for sure! You have to decide for yourself—is becoming an excellent communicator worth the investment? Are you willing to do the work it will take to keep getting better at it? At this stage in your journey into leadership, you should be able to tell how well you are doing with this, but even if you think you have a pretty good idea, I'd like to suggest that you ask around. Check in with a few people who know you well and a few people whom you've been leading already. Ask them how you're doing as a communicator. The work you do on improving this skill will never go to waste.

"The heavens declare the glory of God; the skies proclaim the work of his hands. Day after day they pour forth speech; night after night they display knowledge. There is no speech or language where their voice is not heard. Their voice goes out into all the earth, their words to the ends of the world."

—PSALM 19:1-4

"Do not let any unwholesome talk come out of your mouths, but only what is helpful for building others up according to their needs, that it may benefit those who listen."

—EPHESIANS 4:29

TAKE IT DEEPER

COMMUNICATION: THE DARK SIDE

Our words can bless or they can injure. Proverb 12:18 says, "Reckless words pierce like a sword, but the tongue of the wise brings healing." Some of my worst moments as a leader have resulted from the times when I was reckless with my tongue. I can be wickedly sarcastic at times, and I know I have hurt others, as well as God, by my unwise and hurtful comments. There is a real dark side to communication. Gossip, slander, accusations—we've all been there, hurting someone with our words. Grab that journal and take a few minutes to get real with God about how the dark side of communication sometimes is expressed in you.

JOURNALING SNAPSHOTS

DAY 1

Read Psalm 19:1-6. Record all the ways God has spoken to you through his creation. If you need to, take your Bible and journal outside and then spend some time listening to him.

DAY 2

Read Psalm 19:7-11. How has God spoken to you through his Word? Tell God the ways you've heard him personally speak to you through Scripture.

DAY 3

Read Matthew 15:10-11. Have some unclean things fallen from your lips recently? Where have those things come from? Explore this in your journal writing today.

DAY 4

Read 2 Samuel 12:1-28. Record the different types of communication you see going on in this passage. How would you have handled being on either side of this conversation?

DAY 5

Read James 3. Read through this passage slowly, several times if you need to. Record in your journal the things God brings to mind through James.

CHAPTER EIGHT

THE CONFLICT-MANAGING LEADER

"I urge you to live a life worthy of the calling you have received. Be completely humble and gentle; be patient, bearing with one another in love. Make every effort to keep the unity of the Spirit though the bond of peace."
—Ephesians 4:1-3

Conflict is a part of life, as anyone with a brother or sister can attest to! Do you ever spend time with other people? If you do, then you can expect times of conflict. From minor irritations and misunderstandings to full-blown war, none of us can get away with a conflict-free life. Stepping into the role of a leader will not shield you from conflict—I guarantee it.

In his awesome book *A Work of Heart*, Reggie McNeal writes, "Leadership that is not encountering difficulty is probably not trying to accomplish much." It's easy to think that if you're involved in any kind of conflict, you must have done something wrong or that you're not fit for leadership. Be really careful of this attitude.

Wouldn't it be great if I could give you a magic formula for having a conflict-free life? Life would be so much simpler if only we could all just get along! However, conflict is both a byproduct of our sinful nature as human beings and God's plan for shaping us into the kinds of leaders he wants us to be. God is constantly using people and circumstances to smooth out the rough places in us. By the way, guess who he likes using most for this kind of stuff? You guessed it—our families.

It seems most of us have at least one person in our family whose personality constantly rubs us the wrong way. Have you ever stopped being irritated with that person long enough to consider that God might have put that person in your life to teach you the very thing you need to learn the most (patience, forgiveness, grace)? Think about it—if you were God, and you wanted to teach a person such as you to be more patient or forgiving, how would you do it? What's cool is that God still leaves you a big choice to make—do you let the conflict smooth out a rough spot in you or create a sharper edge? This is one of the many hard decisions a leader has to make.

So I can't give you a magic formula, but I can give you a few things to think about on your journey to becoming the kind of leader who manages conflict with maturity, humility, and courage. Even though every conflict you'll face will be different, there are some components of any conflict that you can think about now.

PREPARE

You're probably thinking, *Wait a minute, most of my conflicts just erupt out of nowhere. How can I prepare for something I don't even know is going to happen?* And of course you are right—to a point. You won't be able to prepare for the specifics of most conflicts, but you can prepare to enter into them in healthy and mature ways.

FIGHT OR FLIGHT?

Remember back in the second chapter when you worked to discover your temperament? It probably revealed to you a little bit about how you are wired to think about conflict. Some of us are wired to run and hide from conflict, avoiding it at all costs. Others are wired to love it. Sometimes people like that will report feeling energized by a "good fight." I have a friend who grew up in a family that argued about politics at the dinner table every night. They yelled, threw stuff, and pounded the table until dessert, when someone would say, "Whose night is it for dishes?" and it was all over. To this day she'll say that most of time she finds arguing fun!

So how are you wired? Are you a "fight" or a "flight"? If you are a flight, you will probably want to ask God regularly for the courage to stay when conflict emerges. Ask yourself, *What happens to me when I sense conflict? Does my heart race? Do I shut down emotionally? Do I give in just to make the conflict go away?* Make a plan for what you will do when you feel those things begin to happen.

If you are a "fight" person, you will want to ask God regularly for gentleness and humility. Ask yourself, *What happens to me when I sense conflict emerging? Do I get louder? Do I use strong language? Do I stop caring about hurting people in my desire to "win"?* You also need to think and pray deeply about these questions and make a plan for what your response should be.

GET OVER YOURSELF

Many of us so dislike conflict that we do everything we can to avoid it, and then we're shocked when it actually happens to us. The truth is, no matter how nice you are or how careful you are to please others, you will experience conflict. Sometimes it will arise out of your attempts to bring about change or from unpopular decisions you make as a leader. Other times your poor judgment or insensitivity will be the cause. Whatever the case may be, accept the fact that conflict is a part of life—and certainly a part of your leadership role—and get over the shock that people may disagree with you. Jesus was perfect in every way, but even he didn't escape conflict. Will you?

YOUR BAD BEHAVIOR

Austin and Bonnie have been the best of friends ever since they met during their freshman year in high school. Both are strong leaders, and they have partnered in many different projects at school and in their church's youth ministry. That's why it shocked everyone when the explosion happened. Austin and Bonnie were in a meeting about an outreach project they were trying to launch at the church. There was a lot of disagreement about some of the key details, and everyone in the room seemed to be talking at once. Austin began to talk louder and louder, obviously trying to gain control of the meeting. Finally, Bonnie interrupted him, "Austin, could you scream at us a little louder, please? We can't hear you!" To which Austin coolly replied, "Well, Bonnie, obviously I have to do *something* to get through your thick skull!" That shut the conversation down in a hurry.

What happened there? Both Austin and Bonnie succumbed to a very common phenomenon. We all have a dark side that comes out when we're stressed. Remember that fight or flight thing? We can't usually flee the room or start punching when things get stressful, so we revert to that dark side and bring out the verbal bad behavior instead. For some the flight mode looks like withdrawing, shutting down into silence, or masking (pretending you feel something you don't). For fight-mode people it could look like name-calling, blaming, defending, or other aggressive behavior. For me it's sarcasm. When I get stressed, I can feel the sarcastic comments start slinging around in my head and fighting to come out of my mouth.

Smart leaders take the time to examine themselves and identify what those tendencies to behave badly under stress-might be. I know that when things get stressful for me, I will most likely be tempted to whip out those sarcastic comments, get defensive, or withdraw completely. None of these are healthy or helpful behaviors, so I have to think through the following questions constantly. I suggest you give them a try as well.

How do I tend to behave badly when I feel stressed?

What things might trigger those reactions?

What will I tell myself when I start to feel these behaviors emerging?

What can I do to keep myself under control?

Have you ever noticed how hard it is to think well when you're in the middle of a conflict with someone? One reason is that God designed our brains to change the way they function when stress is present. That fight-or-flight response is at least partly a brain chemistry thing. In those moments of stress, your blood flow in your brain is diverted more into the brain stem area. Adrenaline is released, and less blood flows to the frontal cortex where the logical thinking takes place. This is just one more reason why you should do some good preparation ahead of time, so when the moment comes, you're ready to behave well.

Does this idea of preparing for conflict ahead of time strike you as a bit weird? I mean, let's be real here—who has time for this stuff? If you ever find you have some extra time on your hands, are you going to spend it catching up on some blog reading, renting that movie you've been waiting to see, or grabbing a journal and doing a bit of meditation about some possible future conflict? Most of us aren't going to choose to work in our journals. Here's the real deal, though: Leadership requires lots of hard choices and sacrifices. The point of this book is to help you along your journey into leadership. Here's a key question for you to consider at this point in your journey: ***If leadership requires me to be willing and able to invest time in getting to know myself well, do I have the right stuff?***

ENGAGE

Of course the time comes when a leader must engage in conflict. It can't—and shouldn't—be totally avoided. When the time comes and you're prepared, you'll be able to be the kind of leader who engages with conflict in a healthy way. Engaging with conflict well doesn't just happen, though. This isn't the time to indulge yourself and let loose all of your frustrations on whomever you happen to have a conflict with. I know it's tempting, but there really is a better way.

KNOW THE RULES!

Fortunately for us the Bible gives us some rules about conflict. There's a lot of stuff in there about how we're supposed to treat people and other things that are related to conflict, but Jesus actually gives us some real rules for getting through conflict.

Grab your Bible and look at Matthew 18. This is the main place where the rules of engagement are listed. (Later on, as you continue on this journey into leadership, you will want to read all of Paul's letters to the churches. He gives us lots of specific directions about relating to each other.) For now let's walk through Matthew 18. Every leader should know verses 15-17 by heart! The rules are pretty simple and can be applied to just about every situation.

"If your brother sins against you, go and show him his fault, just between the two of you. If he listens to you, you have won your brother over." —Matthew 18:15

Rule One: Take Care of It!

If someone has wronged you, you have an obligation to get it taken care of. Don't wait for the other person to come to you. Jesus says you have to take care of it! By the way, this doesn't let you off the hook when you've offended someone else. If you flip back to the fifth chapter of Matthew (verses 23-24), you'll discover that if someone has something against you, the directions are the same—take care of it.

Rule Two: Keep It Private!

This is a hard one. When we've been offended by someone, usually the first thing we want to do is "confide" in someone else. We either want to blow off some steam with someone or try to get some support for our side. It's hard to keep a conflict just between you and the other person, but the right way to do it is to give the other person a chance to make things right before we ever mention it to a third person. There are exceptions to this—like if you feel it would be physically unsafe for you to be alone with the person—but in general, keeping the conflict private protects both of you from gossip and rumor and more damaged relationships.

"But if he will not listen, take one or two others along, so that 'every matter may be established by the testimony of two or three witnesses.'" —*Matthew 18:16*

Rule Three: Bring in a Third Party

This is where a lot of us really blow it. If the private conversation doesn't go so well, it's as if, "Okay, let's go! You've just declared war!" This is where we get *really* tempted to start gossiping and faction-building. It's just way easier to declare the relationship over than to keep working through a process of figuring stuff out. But Jesus is pretty clear about this part of it. When things get heated, people have a hard time being objective about what they're hearing—on *both* sides. If one or both of you brings another person along to join the conversation, there's better accountability for what's really being said and *how* it's being said.

There is another part of this rule that's a bit tricky. Who will that third (or fourth) person be? It's awfully tempting to bring along your best friend, someone you know is on your side. But is he really the best person to bring into the situation? Will he bring wisdom and objectivity? Does he desire truth and peace prevail more than he desires you declared "the winner"? It takes maturity to think through these things when you're in the middle of a chaotic situation, but that's what God expects of his leaders.

"If he refuses to listen to them, tell it to the church; and if he refuses to listen even to the church, treat him as you would a pagan or a tax collector."
—*Matthew 18:17*

Rule Four: Release It

If you've worked through the process with someone—going to them personally and privately first and then bringing another wise person or two to help you sort things out—and you still can't get your conflict resolved, the next step is to let the church handle it. There are a couple of things that are important to realize about this verse. This is one of those places in Scripture that takes a bit more digging to understand.

First of all, in Jesus' day the "church" wasn't the First Methodist on the corner. The "church" was the body of people who followed Christ. For most people that meant a small cluster of families that lived near one another. Jesus didn't mean for us to place an account of our conflict in the church bulletin so everyone could know about it; rather this instruction is meant to sound like this: "Hey, if you guys can't work this out with a couple of helpful people, let the body of believers come around you and help you solve it. Don't take it to court and let the government decide." Jesus is saying we should trust a body of people who are all trying to follow Jesus and live Christlike lives. If someone rejects even that, *then* it's time to release not only the conflict, but also the relationship with that person.

Those four rules—take care of it, keep it private, bring in a third party, and release it—should give you a good structure to follow as you engage with the conflict that comes your way. If you're like me, though, just knowing the rules of the game isn't quite enough. I also want to know the strategies that will help me play well. Even though it's bad practice to view our conflicts as games we want to win (they're not!), it's still good to want to "play" well.

LOOK IN THE MIRROR

Let me ask you this—if you had a big zit on your face, would you want to know it? Of course, it's never fun to take a look in the mirror and spot one of those monsters, but it's better than not looking in the mirror and letting it get bigger and bigger! We all have "zits" on our character, and we never grow as leaders if we choose to protect and keep them.

Several years ago I was involved in a conflict with a friend. I confronted her about the way her behavior was affecting me, and she responded with a laundry list of all of the things that bugged her about me. Her comments were all over the place and had nothing to do with the issue at hand. My initial response was to become defensive and disregard everything she had to say because, after all, this conversation was supposed to be about her. As I thought and prayed about it, though, I realized I had to sort carefully through everything she had said. I realized that if there were even one true thing in the list of problems she had with me, I would want to know it.

Some of the things she listed were simply a matter of personal preference. I do life differently in some ways, and neither her way nor mine is "right." Those comments went into the disregard pile. After some careful consideration I determined there were other things that were simply not true. And then there was the truth pile. I painfully acknowledged she had uncovered some things about me that were true, and I needed to deal with those things. As awkward as it was, I realized I needed to thank her for speaking the truth to me because I would ultimately benefit from having that blind spot revealed. Ouch!

You can deny your own mistakes and shortcomings all day long, but that won't make them go away. And believe me, if you do get away with it, they will pop up again anyway. It's best to do the hard work of searching for the truth in the accusation, deal with it, and grow from it.

FOCUS ON THE CENTER

Okay, imagine you are in a field with another person. You each have a pile of rocks beside you. You can leave your rocks in your piles, or you can put them together and build something new. You can also use those rocks as weapons and throw them at the other person or even try to destroy their pile of rocks with yours. What seems the most productive thing to do?

Now imagine those rocks represent your ideas, viewpoints, and opinions. In a conflict you are tempted to use them to hurt or destroy the other person. You can barricade yourself behind your pile of rocks and start whipping them at your opponent, or you can take a risk and lay them in the center. If the other person does the same thing, pretty soon something new takes shape—something that isn't theirs or yours, but a whole new creation.

Focusing on the center in a conflict means you stop using all of your energy to defend your position or destroy the other person's. It means your main goal is to find common ground and to learn something new. This is how you stop trying to win all of your arguments and learn to manage conflict in a healthy and productive way.

BE KIND AND HONEST

TREAT YOURSELF APPROPRIATELY

In the midst of a conflict it's easy to get down on yourself. Especially as you come to terms with your own mistakes and failings, you need to remember to cut yourself some slack. When there have been leadership mistakes, honestly taking responsibility for them does not indicate failure but success. It's not the absence of conflict in a leader's life that indicates her character; it's how she deals with the conflict. Treating yourself well in the midst of conflict means that when you realize you're lying to yourself ("I'm such a loser…I stink at this leadership stuff…I just can't get along with anyone"), you catch the lies and replace them with truth ("I blew it this time, but I can still take care of it").

TREAT OTHERS APPROPRIATELY

The leader can always afford to be kind and gracious, even (or especially!) in the face of enormous conflict. It's not a sign of weakness but strength. Let's face it: No one really benefits in the long run from being unkind or harsh with someone in a moment of weakness. Most often what feels so good in the moment really just gives us more garbage to apologize for later. Followers need to trust the integrity of their leaders. When they can observe a leader honestly dealing with the truth—without losing his head and treating others harshly—they build trust and loyalty. Honesty without love feels like manipulation or browbeating, and it hurts people. It builds mistrust and hinders any road to forgiveness. I have often regretted my harshness, but I have never regretted being kind to someone in the midst of conflict.

FOLLOW UP

Some leaders get through conflict fine. They size up the situation accurately, keep their cool, negotiate through to the center, and come up with resolution. Then they blow it—they refuse to forgive. How tempting it is to keep that record of wrongs like notches on a belt. The power to forgive is a wonderful gift from God that blesses others by releasing them from the bondage of the past. In a scene from the film *Les Miserables,* the main character, Jean Valjean, takes advantage of the kindness of a bishop who housed him for a night by robbing him. He fills his satchel with silver and sneaks out of the house in the middle of the night. He is soon arrested and brought back to the bishop to be formally charged. Instead of accusing him and ensuring Jean's arrest, the bishop says, "What? I thought I told you to take the candlesticks as well!" The shocked policemen leaves, and the humbled and grateful Valjean turns his life around in that moment of grace, vowing to do good instead of evil for the rest of his life.

Forgiving everyone involved in a conflict—including yourself—is the critical final step to managing conflict. Jesus' last act on earth was to forgive those who took his life. How can we refuse to do something Jesus modeled for us so clearly? It doesn't matter who was right or who was wrong. Managing conflict well includes this final, important step of letting go of the right to use the conflict against anyone.

Have you forgiven the other party in your conflict? How do you know?

Have you forgiven yourself? How do you know?

Do you need to go back and work on forgiving someone for anything that was said or done?

Conflict is never fun, and it's often very painful for everyone involved. The good news is that it can be managed, and we can learn and grow from it. Learning to be a conflict-managing leader rather than a conflict-avoiding leader can mean the difference between your ultimate success or failure in leadership.

JOURNALING SNAPSHOTS

DAY 1

Read Matthew 18:15-17. Have you followed these scriptural guidelines for resolving conflict? Write about the results.

DAY 2

Read the psalm of your choice today. Write a note to God about what this psalm stirs up in you.

DAY 3

Read Ephesians 4:7. Write this verse in your journal, and then write about the grace God has shown you.

DAY 4

Read 1 Timothy 3. How do you match up to this list?

DAY 5

Read Hebrews 12:5-6. How has God disciplined you? Thank him for his loving discipline and for being treated as a son or daughter.

■ CHAPTER NINE

THE MENTORING LEADER

"I know of no leader in any era who hasn't had at least one mentor: a teacher who found things in him he didn't know were there, a parent, a senior associate who showed him the way to be, or in some cases, not to be, or demanded more from him than he knew he had to give."
—*Warren Bennis, On Becoming a Leader*

Throughout this book we've compared the process of becoming a leader to being on a journey. I'd like you to imagine for a moment that you are taking a pilgrimage of a different kind. A little more than a hundred years ago, people were just beginning to settle in the western half of the United States. Thousands of people began their treks as bankers or shopkeepers or teachers, but along the way they became pioneers. Those who not only survived but also thrived during their migration received valuable help and advice from the people who had embarked on this adventure before them. The first groups of pioneers could tell them the best places to cross over rivers and how to hunt and fish the land. Can you imagine how many new things had to be learned on a journey like that?

I think God designed us to need each other. You need someone who is on the journey just ahead of you to hold up a light for you so you can see where you're going, and so you can, in turn, hold up the light for someone else who is coming along behind you. That is what mentoring is all about.

Take a minute and think about your own journey. What people in your life have shined a light for you?

Could you think of at least one name? Take a moment and thank God for what those people have given to you. Shining a light for someone else is an act of service and sacrifice, and it is also a choice.

Somehow our culture has communicated the message that leaders just know it all. Asking for help seems more like weakness than strength. I have a friend who went to an event in which all the participants were blindfolded and sent into a maze. The only instructions were these: "You must find your way out of the maze. If you need help, raise your hand and let us know you need help. Someone will come help you." The trick was that there really was no way out of the maze. But if you raised your hand and said, "I need help," then a person came and guided you outside—that was the solution. And everyone who struggled through and refused to ask for help ended up wandering around aimlessly. When she told me that story, it reminded me of all the leaders I've observed struggling needlessly through the years, all because they refused to accept help from someone who was more than willing to give it.

Being mentored requires humility, not only in accepting the aid of your mentor but also in truly learning from him or her. In order for that relationship to be successful, you need to be able to say three really hard words: "I don't know." Be aware of the temptation to try to impress your mentor with your knowledge. Hiding your ignorance from your mentor is like keeping your symptoms from your doctor. You are in a mentoring relationship to learn, not teach. In this sense you are not equals. Also keep in mind that you are only in this relationship for a brief time, so it's important that you absorb all you can.

How well do you ask for help? What do you need help with right now?

How easily do you admit you have a lot of learning to do?

BEING MENTORED

Are you tracking with this idea? I hope so! Because if you continue on your journey into leadership, there will always be people ahead of you, and there will always be people coming up behind you. Being mentored and mentoring others is something we have to work at doing well. It doesn't usually "just happen." While it's arguably a bit easier to be the one who is being mentored, there are still some things that are important to think about along the way. Here are a few thoughts.

"I'm trying to free your mind, Neo. But I can only show you the door. You're the one that has to walk through it."
—MORPHEUS TO NEO, **THE MATRIX**

THE MENTOR IS NOT YOUR "SAVIOR"

Your mother probably told you no one is perfect. This includes your mentor! It's important that you don't idolize your mentor. He will not be able to teach you every single thing you need to know, and he cannot solve your problems for you. He isn't responsible for your choices, and he isn't responsible for your success. You are. The only perfect mentor is Jesus Christ, and as we are all in the process of being transformed into Christ's likeness, he is the only one we can look to for the answer to every question.

Never stop asking good questions—good questions are often birthed in prayer. Asking meaningless questions that you don't even want the answers to, just for the sake of asking questions or keeping the attention of your mentor, is demeaning and a waste of time for both of you. It's important to invest time in the search for the right questions.

DO YOUR HOMEWORK

If your mentor gives you specific assignments to work on between meetings, honor her by doing them. Follow through on the things your mentor challenges you to do. You will only grow by putting into practice the things you're learning. Don't put it off and then expect to develop simply because you are meeting with a mentor.

LOOK FOR OTHER MENTORS

There is a lot of wisdom in having more than one mentor. Your mentor should never have unlimited influence over you. Too much of any one person, no matter how wise that person is, can be a bad thing. There would be exclusivity of input, and the result is that you would not only pick up your mentor's strengths, but you would also pick up his weaknesses. You are not trying to become a clone. Studies show that, generally speaking, the average person can name five to eight individuals who marked him—people who came into his life at different junctures in time and made a variety of contributions to his life.

PASS IT ON—MENTOR OTHERS

The best reward you can give your mentor is your own growth. As you grow and succeed, begin to look for others to whom you can pass on the gift by mentoring them. Jesus perfected the concept of spiritual multiplication, and it still works today. (A word of caution: It makes for fewer problems and mixed motivations when guys mentor guys and girls mentor girls.)

Abbe Faria: In return for your help in digging this tunnel, I offer you something priceless.

Edmond: My freedom?

Abbe Faria: No, freedom can be taken away, as you well know. I offer you my knowledge.

—THE COUNT OF MONTE CRISTO, ALEXANDRE DUMAS

What things have you learned directly from your mentors?

Have you had a healthy attitude about being mentored—being teachable, not idolizing or draining your mentor, being willing to follow through?

JESUS DID IT—TIMES 12

Many successful leaders consider mentoring the most important of all their responsibilities. Jesus sure seemed to. He invested a lot of his time in those 12 guys. Jesus didn't say a lot about leadership directly. Instead he preferred to model it. We've already looked at how Jesus modeled prayer, servanthood, communication, and cultivating his inner life. Have you noticed how Jesus was intentional about modeling these things not only to the world at large, but also to a few select guys? He took the time to mentor 12 individuals intentionally. For three years they lived life together, and he taught them everything they needed to know to give birth to the church. The message we can take away from Jesus' actions is pretty clear: For kingdom leaders, mentoring isn't an optional addition to the work of leadership—it's an integral part of it.

TOO YOUNG TO MENTOR SOMEONE?

Are you thinking, *Hey, I'm still in school! I can't mentor anyone yet!* Probably the biggest roadblock to this part of your leadership journey is that it's hard to know when you're ready. Here's the deal: You're ready when there is at least one person traveling behind you on the journey. Think about the metaphor I used earlier about shining the light for someone. How far ahead of you do you want that person shining the light for you? So it makes sense that when you're mentoring someone else, you're still on the journey yourself. Mentoring is a process, not an event. If you stop, the other person will quickly pass you by, and then you're not shining the light for him anymore. Mentoring is about relationships—helping each other as you progress toward becoming more Christlike leaders. It's about learning—staying in the learning mode yourself so you have new insights to pass on to others—and learning from one another, and, most importantly, it's about following Christ.

TAKE IT DEEPER

THE EARLY MENTORS

Read 1 Kings 19 to get an inside look at the beginning of the mentoring relationship between Elijah and Elisha. Jot down a few notes about what you notice about their relationship.

MENTORING IS AN INVESTMENT

When I was in my mid-twenties, I worked for a large electronics company. One of the benefits of the job was the opportunity to invest up to 10 percent of your paycheck into stock. I was barely making any money as it was, so it seemed a dumb thing to do at the time, but I decided to bite the bullet and do it. When I left the company, I had quite a few shares of stock that were fully vested. I've hung onto it through the years, and guess what? In the last two years the stock price has gone through the roof and has split twice. I now own four times the shares I started with, and each share is worth more than twice what I paid for it. That initially costly and risky proposition turned out to be a pretty good investment in the end.

Investing in a mentoring relationship isn't much different. You have a limited amount of time, and squeezing in one more relationship probably seems more than you can do. And investing in a mentoring relationship also costs a lot in terms of emotional energy. It's one more thing to think about, work at, and pray about. All relationships take a lot of energy to be successful, and these are no exception. It will cost you something, and it may even cost you a lot.

Are you willing to make the investment? Like my stock investment, it may be a long way down the road before you see the payoff. Are you willing to keep investing in another person even if you don't see any results for a while? Both of you need to have the perspective that you're in this for the long haul. Recently I had the opportunity to see this principle in action in a more personal way. One of the young women whom I have mentored for several years is now leading and mentoring a group of high school girls. I watched her as she was interacting with some of them and marveled as I watched them respond to her. She was like their rabbi! I was watching my investment pay off before my very eyes.

Are you mentoring others? If so, who and how? If not, why not?

What do you know that you could pass on to others?

HOW DO YOU GET STARTED?

Sometimes the beginning of a relationship feels a bit awkward. Especially if you've never really mentored anyone before, it can feel overwhelming when you're not sure where to start. Here are a couple of thoughts to get you going.

BUILD THE RELATIONSHIP

Spending time together, doing things that will help you get to know one another, and having a consistently servant-like attitude are the building blocks to a trusting foundation. And trust is absolutely essential to the relationship. Remember how Lucy tried to teach poor Charlie Brown how to kick a football? Every time he ran and kicked, she jerked the football away at the last minute. Lucy was a lousy mentor. Charlie Brown would never learn from her because he couldn't trust her. The principle is this: Your relationship earns you the right to speak the truth. You cannot change the thinking or behavior of someone who cannot trust that you have his best interests at heart.

AGREE ON THE PURPOSE

If there is anything that will invite disappointment or anger into your mentoring venture, it will be starting out with different expectations. From the beginning you should clearly spell out what you both envision the "end" of your mentoring time to look like. Ask each other, "What do you hope to achieve?" One of the mentor's most important jobs is to seek God regarding the purpose of the relationship. God will often show the mentor a vision for who he wants the person being mentored to become and will help the mentor guide the person toward this vision. The purpose of any mentoring relationship is always some type of personal growth or change for the person being mentored. The specifics of that will be made clear over time and should be freely discussed.

SET UP A PLAN TO CONNECT

How often do you want to meet? Do you want to maintain some of your contact through e-mails and phone calls, or do you need to spend the majority of your time together face to face? Who will initiate contact? How long should each meeting last?

COMMUNICATE ABOUT COMMUNICATION

It'll be helpful to set up some ground rules, so to speak, about how you'll talk with each other. How deep do you want to go? How will you approach disagreements? Will everything be treated as confidential, or only the stuff you specifically ask to be kept just between the two of you? Talking about how you'll talk together not only sets up the relationship to be a healthy one, but it also sets the tone for mutual respect and consideration.

SET AN AGENDA

You wouldn't expect a football coach to show up at practice and ask the players, "So, guys, what do you feel like doing tonight?" Good coaching, like good mentoring, requires a plan. Jesus chose his protégés and then he challenged them with this agenda: "Come, follow me and I will make you fishers of men" (Matthew 4:19). He had specific things in mind that he wanted to teach them in order to accomplish that goal. He taught them how to pray; to cast out demons; to preach and teach; to listen, touch, confront, and forgive. And after he brought them through all of their "fishing lessons," he restated the agenda: "Go and make disciples of all nations, baptizing them in the name of the Father and of the Son and of the Holy Spirit, and teaching them to obey everything I have commanded you" (Matthew 28:19-20).

AS YOU MENTOR, REMEMBER—

STAY TEACHABLE

You cannot impart what you do not possess. Kingdom leaders never finish their training while here on earth. Keep learning, keep seeking, keep growing. Stay connected with others who are mentoring you and always be on the lookout for people who have something to teach you.

LIVE IT!

Try to listen more and talk less. Paul tells the Philippians: "Whatever you have learned or received or heard from me, or seen in me—put it into practice" (Philippians 4:9). Anyone who has ever been to high school knows that people notice the stuff you do and the kind of life you lead. Share your life with those you mentor and allow them to observe you leading and living. They will pick up more from watching you than you could ever think to put into a teaching time.

YOU'RE THE SERVANT, NOT THE MASTER

You've been through chapter 4. 'Nuff said.

Find a person who is actively mentoring someone else. Ask him some of the questions from this chapter and see what you can learn from him about being a good mentor.

DON'T MAKE DECISIONS FOR THOSE YOU MENTOR

Mentoring is not taking responsibility for another's decisions. B.F. Maiz, poet and expert on mentoring, once said, "Good mentoring empowers the person to assume responsibility for themselves. The very essence of good mentoring is to empower people to find ways of solving their own problems, to help people to come to terms with the great contradictions in life" (quoted in *The Mentoring Blueprint,* by Stephen Graves with Thomas G. Addington). You probably know how it feels when someone tries to take over and steal your problems by making decisions for you. It stinks! Wrestling through tough stuff is one of the ways we really grow as leaders. You wouldn't want someone to steal your best learning opportunities from you—why would you want to do that to someone you're trying to help along in her journey?

The concept of mentoring isn't rocket science. It's a beautiful process that Jesus embraced to grow as a leader and develop other leaders. As Jesus is led by the Father, he leads us—"As the Father has loved me, so I have loved you" (John 15:9). We get to follow his example by accepting the light lovingly held out for us by the ones who are ahead of us and by holding out a light behind us for another. What a great idea, huh?

JOURNALING SNAPSHOTS

DAY 1

Read 1 Thessalonians 2:8-10. Have you imparted your very life to others?

DAY 2

Read the Proverb of your choice today. Write a note to God about what this Proverb stirs up in you.

DAY 3

Read Joshua 1. What are you afraid of right now?

DAY 4

Read Acts 17:10-12. Are you following the example of the Bereans? When you have tough questions, are you eagerly searching Scripture for the answers? What are the tough questions you have right now? Write them in your journal and leave room to come back and fill in the answers when you find them.

DAY 5

Read Galatians 1:6-10. In your journal, write down your answers to the questions in verse 10.

■ CHAPTER TEN

PUTTING IT ALL TOGETHER: THE CALL

Phew! You made it to the last chapter! Congratulations on sticking with it. Because you've come this far, you already know the journey into leadership won't be easy every step of the way. It's really important on any kind of journey to stop at intervals and take stock of where you are and where you've been. You've probably heard the phrase, "the beginning of the end." Well, this chapter is really the end of the beginning. Your journey isn't complete—you will likely be on it for a long time to come—but you've already come a long way.

It's time to take a look back at the work you've done and begin to put it all together. I hope you've seen how important it is that you understand the concept of leadership from a biblical perspective and how critical it is for you to do your leading from an integrated heart. I hope you've begun the process of assessing your leadership skills and instilling practices into your life to develop and perfect those skills. We've looked at some of the leadership skills in previous chapters, but of course there are many more. As you continue your journey—and I hope you will continue—God will reveal more and more of who he made you to be and the work he has for you to do.

This brings up a point that many of us struggle with: What work does God want you to do? And how will you know? Moses is the only one I know of who received his assignment from God through a burning bush. For the rest of us, it's a little more complicated.

That godly assignment is often referred to as a "calling." And the calling of God on a person's life is a pretty mysterious thing. But Scripture—and the lives of millions of Christians throughout history—proves that it's a very real phenomenon.

Now just because you've arrived at the last chapter of this book doesn't mean you're supposed to have your calling figured out by now. Maybe you do know, but it's more likely that you don't. And oftentimes God gives us different callings for different seasons in our lives. Some of us receive a calling for our whole lives, but for lots of people that's not the case.

One common misconception is that God only "calls" people into church ministry. I've met lots of people who falsely believe they aren't "serving God" simply because they're working or leading others in the secular world and not in a church or ministry. But nothing could be further from the truth. God calls people to be doctors, lawyers, store clerks—God calls people to serve him everywhere!

My friend Jan is one of my heroes. Jan is a teacher in an inner-city alternative high school. Her students are kids from the roughest neighborhoods, and they all have hard stories to tell. The world has given up on most of these kids. But Jan absolutely loves her job. She knows it's not just a job—it's a calling. Every morning her husband anoints her head with oil and declares her a bearer of Christ. She carries Christ into that classroom with her and allows him to help her see into the hearts of her students. Because of her servant attitude and dedication, she has been able to minister to those kids in countless ways.

As you begin this process of folding together all that you've worked through in the last nine chapters, understand that you *will* receive a calling from God. Jan spent 20 years of preparation doing other things before she landed where she is now. Some of us get our callings at young ages, and others receive them later in life. But no matter when God reveals our calling to us, we can always look back and see that even though we couldn't tell what he was doing, he was busy working on us all along.

"It begins and ends with God, but it loops through a very human individual. It is personal, but bigger than the person. The call comes out of who we are as well as shaping who we are."

—REGGIE MCNEAL, **A WORK OF HEART (EMPHASIS MINE)**

OUR RACE TO THE FINISH LINE

Frequently in the New Testament the image of a race is used as a metaphor for the Christian life. There are many types of races: distance races, sprints, relays—just to name a few. There are many types of races in life as well, and our *calling* is one of the ways we can define the kind of race God intends for us to run. I believe we can better understand our own calling by looking at the way we begin any race: *Ready....Set...Go!*

READY

In any process, people are most likely to skip the step of preparation. It's so tempting to do this, especially when you're in a hurry to get to the "real stuff." Ironically, this is often the most important step. Aren't you glad your doctor didn't skip the eight to 12 years he invested in medical school?

I've suffered the consequences of a lack of preparation. One time I stripped off the wallpaper in my bedroom in preparation for doing some painting. I could see there was still a residue of the wallpaper paste on the walls, but I didn't want to spend days washing and sanding down each wall. (It was a big room!) I figured I could paint right over it, and no one would be able to tell. Well, guess what happened? About six months later the paint started to flake off the walls.

Have you ever experienced that twinge in the pit of your stomach as you looked at a blank test paper and realized you didn't read the right chapter or didn't pay attention in class? The sting of a lack of preparation is pretty sharp in those moments.

Events and tasks that may seem ordinary ultimately work together to build interests or passions in us that eventually turn into our invitations or callings to lead. In the Scriptures we get to read not only the stories about great leaders as they lead, but we also get to see the whole story. No one turns into a great leader overnight. Years and years of preparation go into the making of a leader. If we look at the story of David, we can see he doesn't arrive at the throne of Israel unprepared. The years he spends running from Saul in the desert while leading his ragtag gang of outlaws (who eventually become the "mighty men") shape his heart for leadership in countless ways. Even if we go all the way back to his call into leadership—his anointing by Samuel and his debut in the battle against Goliath—we can see how his years of preparation as a shepherd boy pay off.

Want to see how God prepared some other biblical leaders for their callings? Read the following Take It Deeper section.

TAKE IT DEEPER

GOD PREPARES HIS LEADERS

Grab your Bible and journal. After you've taken a look at these stories, take a minute and record your responses to God in your journal.

Moses was a leader who was assigned the task of getting Pharaoh to release the Israelites from captivity and assemble over a million people for what turned out to be a 40-year journey in the desert.

God prepared Moses by...

- Exodus 2:1-10
- Exodus 2:11-22
- Exodus 3

Samuel was a leader who eventually served as Israel's last judge and was used by God to anoint both Saul and David as kings.

God prepared Samuel by...

- 1 Samuel 1:27-28
- 1 Samuel 2:18-19, 21
- 1 Samuel 2:26

Jesus said Peter was the rock he was going to use to build his church. Peter needed to gather others to follow Jesus Christ and develop those followers into disciples.

God prepared Peter by...

- Mark 1:16
- Matthew 14:28-31
- Matthew 17:1-3

Ask any runner, and he'll tell you the race doesn't begin at the starting line. The race really begins with every one of those daily decisions to practice and prepare for the day of the race. You may not have sensed your calling into leadership yet, but if you've arrived at this point in the book, you are most certainly in the preparation process.

Take a few minutes and go back to the beginning of the book. Look through each chapter, reviewing your responses to some of the questions.

How has what you've learned about building a heart of integrity helped prepare you for leadership?

Look carefully at chapter 2. How has the wiring God equipped you with helped prepare you for leadership? What strengths will help you as a leader?

Have you started to practice some leadership skills intentionally? How have you started to work on strengthening these areas?

What experiences has God given you to practice?

SET

"Because the sovereign Lord helps me, I will not be disgraced. Therefore have I set my face like flint, and I know I will not be put to shame."
—Isaiah 50:7

At some point in the life of every leader, the decision must be made to answer the call to leadership. Even though the practice of ongoing learning will never end, the formal time of preparation has come to an end. It's race day!

This call takes many forms. For some it's a clear invitation into a leadership position. For others it's a more subtle process—but one that ends in a decision to influence others in a personal way. For instance, you may be invited or feel compelled to run for office in your school government. Or your passion about an issue or cause may propel you into standing up for your beliefs, which could lead to influencing others into action. Either way, the time comes when you must make a decision to act. When you watch a race, you notice the runners gather at the starting line and spend the last few moments continuing their preparation. Some will stretch; others will jump around; while still others seem to be just nervously waiting. At some point a voice announces that the race is beginning. The runners need to pay attention—to listen for that call—and then they need to respond by getting into position.

Remember in chapter 6 about how Samuel received his call? Samuel, probably a young teen, is lying down one night when God calls his name. He thinks it is Eli in the next room. So he runs in and says, "Here I am. You called?" Eli probably snorted and sighed impatiently before replying, "No, I didn't. Go back to bed." This happens three times before Eli wakes up enough to realize Samuel is hearing *something*, and if it isn't him, then it is probably God. Eli instructs Samuel to go back to bed, keep listening, and, when he hears the voice again, to say, "Speak, Lord, your servant is listening."

Isn't that just like most of us? God is trying to get our attention—he wants to give us an assignment—and sometimes it takes us a while to wake up and realize he is talking to us. Hearing God's call means maintaining a heart that says, "Speak, Lord, your servant is listening." Often when I lie in bed at night or when I sit down with my journal in the morning, I will say this out loud and wait for God to speak to me. Most of the direction I have received from God in my leadership journey has come during these times.

What is God saying to you? Is he prompting you to use your influence in a particular area?

Hearing the call is one thing, but responding to it is another. The response calls for a decision. For years David had been preparing by watching over his father's flocks of sheep in the dangerous mountain wilderness. He's been slinging stones at predators who tried to attack the flock, all the while honing and perfecting his skills. The preparation for his moment with Goliath is done. When he is sent to the battlefield to bring lunch to his brothers, he encounters the call. Something in his spirit must have clicked when he hears Goliath spewing threats at the Israelite army. He could have waited around and watched to see what the Israelite warriors were going to do. He also could have turned on his heels and run away. Read his actual response: "David said to Saul, 'Let no one lose heart on account of this Philistine; your servant will go and fight him'" (1 Samuel 17:32). He responds with a yes. At that moment he sets his heart on answering God's call. Let's take another look at some of our scriptural leaders and their responses to God's call.

How does Moses respond? (Exodus 4:13)

The prophet Jeremiah? (Jeremiah 1:6)

Jonah? (Jonah 1:3)

How about Gideon? (Judges 6:17)

What about Peter? (Matthew 4:20)

As you can see, it's not always easy to set your heart when you first hear the call. As you look at the responses of Moses, Jeremiah, Jonah, and Gideon, what is the common ingredient to their resistance to God's call? Fear. They were afraid they'd fail because of their age, lack of talent, social position, or lack of experience. And poor old Jonah had a pretty nasty attitude problem as well.

What fears may prevent you from responding well to God's call on your life?

How is your attitude? Are you willing to serve God however he asks you to?

I laminated the following statement on a card and carried it with me for years. "Until I am committed, there is a hesitancy, a chance to draw back. But the moment I definitely commit myself, then God moves also, and a whole stream of events erupts. All manner of unforeseen incidents, meetings, persons, and material assistance, which I could never have dreamed would come my way, begin to flow toward me—the moment I make a commitment."

—DR. JOHN C. MAXWELL, **LEADERSHIP WIRED E-NEWSLETTER** (MARCH 2001)

I love God's response to these guys. Only two—David and Peter—respond with an immediate yes. Does God give up and move on? No, he responds back with a mixture of love, patience, gentleness, and discipline. Moses' whining eventually drives God to anger, but he still lovingly insists that Moses is his guy. I love the assurance that even though I may not respond perfectly, God will not give up on me, either. He may have to discipline me to bring me into compliance (and he has!), but he gets me there all the same. We get a wonderful reminder of this in Philippians 1:6: "He who began a good work in you will carry it on to completion until the day of Christ Jesus." When God begins the work of preparation for leadership in your life, he will finish it.

When we set our hearts on something, we are determining to do it. We are making a firm decision, setting a direction. David repeatedly says in the Psalms that he "set his heart" on God's Word. If the runner does not set in the right direction, he will waste precious energy and time correcting his path. If he doesn't set at all, he will not get a good start and will likely not finish well. That brings us to the next step.

GO!

Once you've set your face toward the call and told God yes, it's time to run. It's tempting to think that just because God has given you the gifts, the passion, and even the clear calling to do something that it's going to be a piece of cake. Think again! Living out your calling takes courage, determination, perseverance, and a constant yielding to the will of God. At the same time, when God *anoints* you for a certain purpose, there is a Spirit-empowered ability and desire present that will often provide that same courage, determination, perseverance, and ability to obey.

I have heard God's call in my life a lot, and sometimes I blow it off. But there was one time when I had nowhere to go in my life. My mom was just diagnosed with an illness. My dad had just had his hip replaced. My sisters were young and didn't understand what was going on. My dad owns a food pantry. But since he was hurt, the place was closed. That meant a lot of people were left without food. One night I was ready to go to sleep, and I started to pray.

Watching the graceful runner break out of the gate and glide toward the finish line can give us a false sense of security about this stage of the race. What we often don't see are the countless times the runner tripped or hit the hurdle while trying to run to victory. We'd like to think that after the work of preparation and decision-making is finished, it's smooth sailing from then on. The truth is that there *will* be hurdles, and they'll come in all different sizes and shapes and at different intervals along the way.

I asked God to watch over our family and the food pantry. The next day I can't describe the feeling I felt. I wanted to make a difference. I went to my dad in the hospital and said, "I'm going to open the food pantry." That week the pantry was open, and my dad took his first step with his new hip.

—JAMES W., 13

Many of the hurdles are those you've looked at already in your journey. You know you have weaknesses in your temperament, and you don't have all the gifts. You know you won't always serve perfectly. You'll forget to pray. You know that if you don't tend to your inner life, you'll get out of balance and succumb to some real leadership killers such as jealousy, lying, or pride. Conflict will come your way, and miscommunication will happen. These are the things for which you've begun to prepare. And there will be others.

Does the fact that there will be hurdles along the way discourage you from running the race? Let me just encourage you with this: You can do it! God will give you the strength and the courage to face every hurdle. Sure, sometimes you'll fall, but just think of what happens to the crowd when a runner who stumbles picks himself up and keeps running. Think of the cheers in the heavenly realm when you do the same.

The "Go!" part of running the race is a wonderful, exciting, challenging thrill. Despite the obstacles, when we are running the course that God designed for us, there is nowhere else we'd rather be. I once met with a student leader who was sensing God's call to leadership for the first time. God had been preparing her for a long time, but she'd never really seen it. Suddenly, she was given an opportunity to lead, and she cautiously stepped into it. Before long she was seeing fruit. Not everything was perfect—there were a few challenges—but I will never forget what she said to me as she described what she was doing. She said, "It's as if I were born to do this!" She was positively glowing. I could relate. There is nothing better than experiencing the thrill of answering God's call and walking in his anointing.

RESPONDING TO THE CALL

Where are you in the process? Are you in the "ready" phase? If you are, then dive into it with everything you have. Much of what you are learning may seem irrelevant to you now, but God knows what he's doing. Be watching and listening for God's direction. Learn all you can. Pray with all your heart, serve whenever the opportunity arises, learn to listen and communicate as well as you can, carefully tend to your inner life, take care of conflicts with others, and follow a good leader. There are many other ways that God is preparing you for leadership—too many for me to list. God's recipe for preparing you is as unique as the call he has for you. It's up to you to submit to the preparation and do your part.

Author Reggie McNeal writes in *A Work of Heart*, "God's part of the call dynamic is to initiate, guide, position, and intervene. The leader's part of the call drama is to hear, respond, search, and order or reorder life." If you are in this stage, the enemy may be trying to tell you that you aren't a leader because you aren't experiencing leadership. Don't worry—David's brothers told him the same thing. They were wrong, too.

If you are in the "set" phase, you may feel a wrestling in your spirit as you try to discern whether you are truly hearing from God. This is an important place to get godly counsel—but not too much. Don't be tempted to talk to people more than you talk to God about it and don't make the mistake of getting too much advice. Stick to one or two trusted, mature advisors—people who will pray with you and listen well. Ultimately, this is a place between you and God. He calls, you answer. God is always the initiator. Often in this phase the enemy likes to come in and remind us of all the reasons why God couldn't possibly be asking us to do what we think he is. We remember our past failures, and our fear of new things comes flying in. Take a look at the first chapter of Joshua or chapter 28 of 1 Chronicles. Both Joshua and Solomon are in the same boat. Can you imagine getting the call from God to take over from Moses? Or King David? Yikes! God is so good to Joshua and Solomon—he reminds them over and over again to have courage and that he'll always be with them. If you are hearing a call from God, don't let fear stop you. "Speak, Lord, your servant is listening."

If you are in the "Go!" phase, then you are already leading. Much of your time will be spent doing the same thing you did in the "ready" phase—learning. You can never stop. As John C. Maxwell says, "A leader who stops learning stops leading." This may be the last chapter of this leadership-training manual, but you are far from finished learning about leadership. Your job is to "be strong and do the work" (1 Chronicles 28:10) with the goal of finishing well. Your greatest challenge will be to keep your focus intact—simply doing the will of the One who called you.

There is an old story about a preacher who had a dream in which he was preaching before a large crowd. He preached the best sermon he'd ever preached. It had come from the very depths of his being. When he finished, he waited for the applause of the audience. The room was silent. Then he heard clapping. It was coming from one person, up in the back of the balcony. Squinting his eyes against the harsh stage lighting, he looked up, trying to see who was applauding him. To his amazement he saw it was Jesus.

As you run the leadership race, never forget that you won't please every person. You won't do all of it right all the time. You probably won't even do it better than everyone else. But you are running to the finish line for the One who will be standing there, waiting to greet you with, "Well done, good and faithful servant" (Matthew 25:21, 23). *That is the prize.*

JOURNALING SNAPSHOTS

DAY ONE

Read Matthew 4:18-20. What is your honest response to God when he asks you to follow him? Write out a recent dialogue between you and God.

DAY TWO

Read Luke 22:31-32. Can you imagine Jesus praying for your faith? Meditate on this verse and journal your response.

DAY THREE

Read John 6:22-29. Write out a list of things you believe. Are most of them easy or difficult to believe? Jesus said that believing in him is the work God requires of us. Is this easy or hard work for you? Reflect on these things in your journal today.

DAY FOUR

Read 1 John 2:27. What has your anointing taught you?

DAY FIVE

Read Romans 8:5. Today examine the things your mind is set on and reflect on them in your journal.

The Circle Maker, Student Edition

Dream Big. Pray Hard. Think Long.

Mark Batterson with Parker Batterson

Pray Circles Around Your Greatest Dreams and Biggest Fears

Prayer can sometimes be a frightening thing—how do you approach the maker of the world, and what exactly can you pray for? In this student adaptation of *The Circle Maker*, Pastor Mark Batterson uses the true legend of Honi the circle maker, a first-century Jewish sage whose bold prayer saved a generation, to uncover the boldness God asks of us at times, and what powerful prayer can mean in your life. Drawing inspiration from his own experiences as a circle maker, as well as sharing stories of young people who have experienced God's blessings, Batterson explores how you can approach God in a new way by drawing prayer circles around your dreams, your problems, and, most importantly, God's promises. In the process, you'll discover this simple yet life-changing truth:

> God honors bold prayers; bold prayers honor God. And you're never too young for God to use you for amazing things.

Available in stores and online!

The Ultimate Guide to Being a Christian in College

Don't Forget to Pack Your Faith

Jeff Baxter

Are You Ready for the Rest of Your Life?

You got the high school diploma, received the college acceptance letter, and have your eye on that dorm fridge. Everything seems new and exciting—but with those positive feelings come huge questions about what awaits you once you're no longer home but sharing a small room with strangers instead. Don't fear! Here is your essential guide for everything you need to know to survive and thrive, with tips on:

- Dorm life
- Dealing with professors
- Selecting classes
- Balancing school and fun
- Standing firm in your faith
- Becoming who you're meant to be
- And more!

With godly wisdom and understanding, Jeff Baxter draws from his experience helping young adults like you build a solid foundation for your life ahead.

Available in stores and online!

Not a Fan: Teen Edition

What does it mean to really follow Jesus?

Kyle Idleman

If someone asked, "Are you a fan of Jesus?", how would you answer? You attend every movie featuring a certain actor, you know the stats of your sports hero, and you can recite lyrics from your favorite songs. In short, you're a huge fan. But are you treating Jesus the same as the other people you admire? The truth is Jesus wants more than the church attendance, occasional prayer, and the ability to recite Scripture—the fan response. He's looking for people who are actually willing to sacrifice in order to follow him. In this teen edition of *Not a Fan*, Kyle Idleman uses humor, personal stories, and biblical truth as he challenges you to look at what it means to call yourself a Christian and follow the radical call Jesus presents. So, will you be a fan, or a follower?

Available in stores and online!